Welcome

Hello and welcome to this special issue of *Airports of the World*. Way back in 2013, I spotted a request for reader submissions in *Airports of the World* and after pondering my self-doubt for a few days, I thought 'what the heck' and emailed in my idea. I was astonished to receive a reply, even more so that it was positive, and so the concept of 'Flying Visits' was born. After visiting Berlin/Tegel and writing up my copy I sent it in still expecting to receive the knockback I was certain was coming. A reply duly came, and again I was astonished, I was being published in the September/October 2013 issue of the magazine. One article proposed, one article written, one article published – if only life was so simple!

Back then I was thrilled to see myself in print, and a dozen years later I have the honour of helming the return to flight status of this title. Having first hit the news stands in the autumn of 2005, the most recent and 100th issue of *Airports of the World* was the March/April 2022 issue. Readers we have met at aviation fairs over the last year or so have told us this is the title they missed – we've listened – so here it is: as we enter our 20th anniversary, we present a packed, 116-page, bumper issue.

Richard Schuurman studies the relationship between KLM and Amsterdam/Schiphol where the prospect of a reduction in aircraft movements is the subject of fierce debate. Elsewhere in Europe we report from Vienna, and detail the expansion of Venice/Marco Polo. Lee Cross describes the rise and fall of the not so mythical Don Quijote Airport, built to relieve pressure on Madrid/Barajas but now operating without any scheduled traffic.

Closer to home, we have features on the symbiosis between the airports at Land's End and St Mary's, plus Southampton's runway extension and, revolutionary for its time, the Eurohub at Birmingham Airport. Flying Visits returns, this time with ABC trips to Ajaccio and Bermuda, that's aviation, beaches and culture. Thomas Haynes has been to Phoenix Sky Harbor and Flagstaff to learn more about their operations, while our Stateside correspondent, Chris Sloan, has been to the far end of Florida for the opening of Concourse A at Key West International Airport.

We've also got features on Japan's game-changing Kansai Airport as it celebrates its 30th birthday, and what might become the world's largest airport in the next few years – Dubai/Al Maktoum. We also look into the complex subject of passenger psychology within the airport environment, examining what can be done to improve the traveller experience. Plus all the significant airport news from the last 12 months and a word about drop-off fees!

If you have a burning question or comment about *Airports of the World* to share with our global audience, do get in touch via airlinerworld@keypublishing.com with the subject 'Letters to the Editor'.

One final note before this issue departs: if you haven't already, do consider a subscription for *Airliner World* – it's the best-value way to enjoy our monthly magazine stablemate. You'll receive your copy ahead of the pack, delivered free to your door, and enjoy discounts on a range of other aviation goodies. A first-class service at an economy-class price!

Wherever you are in the world, and whichever airport you are headed to and through, I hope you enjoy this issue.

Robert Veitch
Assistant Editor, *Airliner World*

While Don Quijote Airport experienced a turbulent decade, Madrid/Barajas went from strength to strength, with the opening of Terminal 4 in 2006 to becoming the fifth busiest airport in Europe by 2024 *AENA*

"

FEATURES

this issue

SCENIC FLIGHTS
34

12

52

WELCOME TO THE CONCH REPUBLIC
WELCOME TO KEY WEST
70

46

ISBN: 978 1 83632 113 2
Editor: Robert Veitch
Editor (Airliner World): Thomas Haynes
Assistant Editor: Lee Cross
Senior editor, specials: Roger Mortimer
Email: roger.mortimer@keypublishing.com
Cover Design: Steve Donovan
Design: SJmagic DESIGN SERVICES, India
Advertising Sales Manager: Sam Clark
Email: sam.clark@keypublishing.com
Tel: 01780 755131
Advertising Production: Becky Antoniades
Email: Rebecca.antoniades@keypublishing.com

SUBSCRIPTION/MAIL ORDER
Key Publishing Ltd, PO Box 300,
Stamford, Lincs, PE9 1NA
Tel: 01780 480404
Subscriptions email: subs@keypublishing.com
Mail Order email: orders@keypublishing.com
Website: www.keypublishing.com/shop

PUBLISHING
Group CEO: Adrian Cox
Publisher: Steve O'Hara
Published by
Key Publishing Ltd, PO Box 100,
Stamford,
Lincs, PE9 1XQ
Tel: 01780 755131
Website: www.keypublishing.com

PRINTING
Precision Colour Printing Ltd, Haldane,
Halesfield 1, Telford, Shropshire. TF7 4QQ

DISTRIBUTION
Seymour Distribution Ltd, 2 Poultry Avenue,
London, EC1A 9PU
Enquiries Line: 02074 294000.

86

94

The stories that shaped global aviation hubs

Airports of the World shines a light on some of the biggest airport news stories of the year

London calling

The seemingly neverending debate regarding airport expansion in the UK continued to rumble on. **Heathrow's** bid for a third runway was given the seal of approval by Chancellor of the Exchequer Rachel Reeves in January 2025, with the intention to proceed during the current parliamentary term and aiming to being operational by 2040. In the meantime, the London gateway, which handled 83.9 million passengers in 2024 and is currently the busiest airport in Europe, is likely to lose the crown to Istanbul sooner rather than later. In other news, the Civil Aviation Authority capped airline landing fees at Heathrow, reducing them to £23.72 per passenger in 2025 and £23.70 for 2026, saying this reflected the anticipated rebound of passenger numbers to pre-COVID-19 levels. Elsewhere, after four years, Heathrow finally returned to profit in 2023, recording an adjusted pretax profit of £38m, compared to a £684m loss during 2022, when it was forced to impose a passenger cap after staff shortages.

Gatwick announced plans to convert its existing emergency northern runway, 08L/26R, into an active runway. It is currently in a period of consultation with regard to noise mitigation and public transportation improvements and is said to be 'spade ready', with a decision due in October 2025. The change of use forms part of a £2.2bn expansion project that would see Gatwick capable of handling 75 million passengers per year by the late 2030s. If it goes ahead, the Sussex hub will eventually lose its status as the busiest single-runway airport in the world. In other news, the facility announced updated plans for the £140m extension of its mid-airfield Pier 6, adding eight new aircraft gates with a capacity for 7.5 million passengers per year. This, in turn, will remove the need to coach 500,000 passengers to remote stands, cutting 12,000 bus journeys. The project is expected to be completed during 2027.

Stansted announced a £1.1bn five-year investment programme, of which the centrepiece is a £600m expansion of the airport's existing terminal building to create "a bright, spacious environment, with more seating areas plus new shops, bars and restaurants." The remaining £500m will be spent on creating an enlarged security hall and installing next-generation security equipment, creating an on-site solar farm, reconfiguring the gate room to create more space for passengers, refurbishing toilet facilities and upgrading the airfield taxiway. Three bays will be added to the back of the current terminal building, extending its overall footprint by 16,500m² and expanding airport capacity up to 43 million passengers per year.

Expansion plans submitted by **Luton** were approved by the UK government on April 3, 2025, with the airport looking to double its annual passenger numbers to 32 million by 2043. Its owner, Luton Rising, said the move could bring "significant economic, employment and social benefits" for the town. The plans include a new terminal building, additional aircraft stands, new taxiways, improvements to the existing terminal and developments in current infrastructure and facilities. The airport said the expansion had "some of the most robust, far-reaching and comprehensive commitments to sustainability introduced at a UK airport."

Plans to increase capacity at **London/City** from 6.5 to 9 million passengers per year, with additional early morning flights, have already been given the green light. ⤵

As Heathrow's largest airline, British Airways stands to significantly benefit from any expansion project *Vincenzo Pace*

Gatwick Airport plans to convert its existing emergency northern runway, 08L/26R, into an active runway
Gatwick Airport

Ground-breaking took place at the $10bn Singapore/Changi Terminal 5 in May 2025
Changi Airport Group

Around the UK

Bristol Airport unveiled its master plan to 2040 "to meet the strong and growing demand of people in the region using the airport." Its consultation document included plans to increase passengers numbers from 12 to 15 million per year, with aircraft movements rising from 85,990 to 100,000 annually. Other points include a terminal extension, new hotel, new taxiways, increasing the number of aircraft parking stands from 38 to 48 and an 150m runway extension to allow "longer-range aircraft, serving a limited number of long-haul destinations and more efficient short-haul flights." The facility is already investing £400m to improve the customer experience and reduce carbon emissions.

Having sat empty since its closure in November 2022, **Doncaster Sheffield** could be set to open its doors again as soon as spring 2026. It first opened for commercial flights in April 2005, but closed in November 2022 after owners,

Peel Group, decided the facility was no longer financially viable, having failed to make a profit in its 17-year history. However, City of Doncaster Council has fought to reopen the facility, signing a 125-year lease on the site. In February 2025, it emerged that Munich Airport International (MAI), the German airport's management and consultancy arm, will provide "operational and management services" to the facility. The council has also established a new company, FlyDoncaster, to oversee the facility's running, and is awaiting news on the reinstatement of the airport's airspace. At its peak, aircraft operated to more than 50 destinations and it handled more than a million passengers per year.

In April 2025, **Birmingham Airport** announced a £10m investment to expand and upgrade its arrivals area, allowing it to process up to eight arriving flights per hour. Projects include the addition of another baggage carousel at a cost of £4.2m and the installation of three new Border Force control desks, along with

a larger immigration hall to process arriving passengers in the 'south' arrivals area.

During April 2025, work commenced on a new passenger terminal at **Blackpool**, planning permission having been granted the previous September. The development will offer an enhanced arrivals and departures area, as well as a larger security checkpoint to host new X-ray and scanning equipment. It will allow the airport to grow the number of corporate aircraft, executive and charter flights it can handle, up to 45 passengers at a time. Commercial traffic at the facility ceased in October 2014 and the previous passenger terminal was later demolished.

Cornwall Airport Newquay, which handled 415,989 passengers and 20,000 aircraft movements in 2024, announced a three-year partnership with Airport Coordination Ltd (ACL) in January 2025 to enhance its operations through data collection services. ACL is the world's first independent slot co-ordinator and provides schedule facilitation and data collection services to airports worldwide. Newquay became its 27th airport in the UK and 76th worldwide.

Newcastle International Airport unveiled plans for a major new cargo hub in March 2025, which could create up to 1,400 direct jobs and boost the regional economy by £165m annually. Officially named AirLink, the 750,000sq ft site will serve as "a key hub for cargo operators, freight forwarders and ground handling agents." Management said that the new facility would play a crucial role in developing the airport's growing cargo operation, which handled a record 6,000 tonnes last year. The plan is to build the new facility south of the runway, offering direct apron access for cargo aircraft, and close to the A1 to ensure freight can be moved onwards quickly. The airport expects

to submit a planning application for the development later this year.

The £100m terminal regeneration at **Leeds Bradford** is set to be completed in summer 2025, offering an 83% expansion in terminal capacity. Once the new extension is open, attention will turn towards the upgrade of the existing terminal.

One of those days

UK airports were thrown into chaos after a nationwide issue caused 270 automated e-gates located at 15 air and rail ports across the UK to fail at 1944hrs on Tuesday, May 7, 2024. The Home Office said that "a large-scale contingency response" was implemented within six minutes. UK Border Force officials had to process passengers manually, creating long queues at airports. The e-gates came back online shortly after midnight, but this was the second time the system had failed due to technical issues, having previously done so over the Spring Bank Holiday weekend in 2023.

On July 19, 2024, a global computer outage at US cybersecurity company CrowdStrike caused chaos as thousands of flights were delayed or cancelled, leaving countless customers affected. Those lucky enough to travel were issued with handwritten boarding cards, while airport staff escorted passengers to their gates as information displays failed. According to the aviation analytics firm Cirium, a total of 6,855 worldwide flights were cancelled on the day of the outage, equating to 6.2% of all scheduled flights. The disruption continued over the weekend and into the following week.

Heathrow suffered a fire at an electrical substation in Hayes on the night of March 20, 2025, which led to the airport's full closure until around 1800hrs

Above: Doncaster Sheffield could be set to open its doors again as soon as spring 2026 *Doncaster Sheffield Airport*

Left: Tampa International Airport hopes its 16-gate Airside D facility will become a premier passenger experience when it opens in 2028 *Tampa International Airport*

Going digital

In July 2024, Norwegian airport operator Avinor revealed it would be adding seven new facilities across Norway to its remote tower programme. The airports set to benefit from the latest technology include **Båtsfjord, Vadsø, Sørkjosen, Sandane, Mosjøen, Ørsta Volda** and the new airport in **Mo i Rana**. An eighth installation at **Bodø Airport**, due to open in 2029, is also part of the agreement. Norwegian defence and aerospace giant Kongsberg, with whom Avinor has worked closely on the programme since 2015, is supplying the digital towers, which are expected to be operational from 2027. Avinor is responsible for 43 state-owned airports in Norway, as well as the air traffic control for commercial and military aviation across the country. **Sønderborg Airport** in Denmark will become the first in the country to implement a remote air traffic control system, using SAAB digital air traffic solutions technology. Its implementation will allow the airport to improve operational efficiency and remove the need to build a new physical tower while retaining local air traffic control jobs. The move forms part of Sønderborg's DKK212m (£24.2m) transformation plan, as the facility looks to become a key aviation hub for southern Denmark.

the following day, disrupting more than 270,000 passengers. While back-up systems did activate, it took around ten hours to reconfigure the airport's tech to run from two other substations. CEO Thomas Woldbye defended the decision to close the airport, saying that keeping Heathrow open during this time would have caused serious issues with a potential risk to life.

Infrastructure projects

In January 2024, Spanish Prime Minister Pedro Sánchez revealed that **Adolfo Suárez Madrid Barajas Airport** would receive a €2.4bn investment as part of expansion plans to make the facility Europe's primary gateway to Latin America and to develop connections to Asia. The ambitious project will

DON'T MISS OUT ON OTHER KEY AVIATION MAGAZINE SPECIALS

If you'd like to be kept informed about Key Publishing's aviation books, magazine specials, subscription offers and the latest product releases. **Scan here »»**

see existing terminals refurbished and expanded, but no new ones built. During 2024, 66.2 million passengers used the gateway and the works aim to increase capacity to 90 million passengers per year by 2031.

In May 2024, Portuguese Prime Minister Luís Montenegro announced that Lisbon's new airport would be located at the military airfield in Alcochete, around 25 miles east of the city. Named **Luís de Camões**, the two-runway gateway will eventually become the capital's only airport, replacing the current **Humberto Delgado**, with a planned opening date of 2034. It will be designed with space for two further runways and a maximum capacity of 100 million passengers per year. To make the new facility more accessible from the city, a new bridge will be constructed across the Tagus river. The ambitious project is estimated to cost in the region of €9bn and, during the construction phase, Humberto Delgado will be expanded to facilitate increased demand. Opponents had argued for the opening of the military air base at Montijo for low-cost flights to operate as a dual-hub with the current airport.

As part of its Vision 2030, the Saudi Arabian government plans to increase its aviation network to reach 250 destinations from Saudi Arabia, and carry more than 330 million passengers annually. The programme includes the construction of a new airport in the capital city Riyadh. Known as **King Salman International Airport**, it is expected to become the physically largest in the world, covering around 22 square miles with six parallel runways, capable of handling 130 million passengers by 2030. Other projects include the expansion of **Abha International Airport**, where plans include a new Foster + Partners designed 20-gate terminal with capacity for 13 million passengers per year.

Ethiopian Airlines will eventually move to a new home hub after plans for a new mega airport located 25 miles southeast of the carrier's existing home at **Addis Ababa/Bole**, were announced. Featuring an 11,840,306sq ft terminal, it is projected to have the capacity to serve 110 million passengers annually, four times that of Bole. The first phase of the new loan-funded **Abusera International Airport**, with an initial

capacity for 60 million passengers, and costing a reported $6bn, is scheduled for completion in 2029. The news came on the back of Qatar Airways' 60% stake in Rwanda's new **Bugesera Airport**, 25 miles south of Kigali, and due to open in 2027.

Groundbreaking took place at the $10bn **Singapore/Changi** Terminal 5 in May 2025. The terminal, with a capacity for 50 million passengers per year, is expected to become operational in the middle years of the next decade. The 1,080 hectare development on reclaimed land includes a new third runway and will become the home of **Singapore Airlines** and its subsidiaries as they coalesce in a single terminal.

Melbourne Airport gained approval from the Australian government for a third runway which it said would deliver "much needed aviation infrastructure capacity for Victoria and help support thousands of new jobs." The 9,840ft strip will be built parallel and 0.8 miles west of the existing north-south runway 16/34, with a planned opening in 2031. Elsewhere in Australia, construction at the new **Western Sydney Airport** is ongoing, with the facility due to become operational in late 2026.

Hong Kong International Airport began operating its new three-runway system at the end of November 2024, which will enable the hub to eventually accommodate 120 million passengers and 10 million tonnes of cargo, cementing its role as a key global aviation centre. The £12.5bn project began in 2016, with the new north runway completed in 2022. Reconfiguration of the centre runway included upgrades such as new taxiways and safety systems.

Plans for a new £8.7bn international hub in Poland moved a step closer after the country's government decided on a location for the central multimodal transport infrastructure project. Currently named **Centralny Port Komunikacyjny**

Hong Kong International Airport began operating its new three-runway system at the end of November 2024
Cathay Cargo

(Central Communication Port), it includes a new airport, high-speed rail links and road connections and will be strategically located between the Polish capital, Warsaw, and the city of Łódź. Construction of the two-runway facility, with initial capacity for 34 million passengers per year, is due to begin in 2026, with opening expected in 2032.

Only in America

Last December, **Tampa International Airport** broke ground on its new $1.5bn 16-gate Airside D facility, which the US hub predicts will be a premier passenger experience when it opens in 2028. The airport said it will operate on two levels, including a mezzanine housing two airline lounges offering views of the airfield. It will contain an international arrivals processing area, a shuttle link to the main terminal, shopping and dining with 360° views of the gates, open spaces, intuitive wayfinding and natural light. The previous Airside D was demolished in 2007, making this new build the hub's first airside expansion in almost two decades.

Work continues at **Chicago/O'Hare** with the installation of taxiway upgrades, airport roads and the creation of three new temporary gates at Concourse C, in readiness for the construction of the Satellite 1 Concourse. Connected to Concourse C (Terminal 1) via a bridge,

the building has been inspired by the orchard that gave O'Hare its original name, Orchard Field, and will provide 19 additional gates for both international and domestic flights.

Elsewhere in the US: The Mickey Leland International Terminal at **Houston/George Bush**, consolidating Terminals D and E, opened in October 2024 with six new widebody gates. The new $1.57bn terminal at **Pittsburgh International Airport** is said to be the first "from the ground up" terminal in the US since COVID-19 and is likely to open late in 2025. Work on the second part of **Portland International Airport's** new tree-lined terminal is expected to finish in 2026. At **Los Angeles International Airport** renovations to Terminal 4 and 5 are ongoing in advance of the 2028 LA Olympic Games, while improvements to Terminal 6 are expected to be completed in 2025. At **San Francisco International Airport**, the modernisation of Terminal 3 West is ongoing through to 2029. Work at **New York/JFK** to upgrade Terminals, 1, 4 and 6 is continuing, opening in stages through to 2030. And finally at **Austin-Bergstrom International Airport,** the West Gate Terminal Concourse B expansion will be completed no earlier than 2030. ✈

Lisbon/Humberto Delgado will close when the new Lisbon/Luís de Camões opens in 2034
Vinci Concessions

Expansion plans at Luton were approved by the UK government on April 3, 2025, and include a new terminal, eventually raising capacity to 32 million passenger per year by 2043 *Luton Airport*

FEATURE

PHX

PHOENIX SKY HARBOR

UNITED STATES

airports of the world

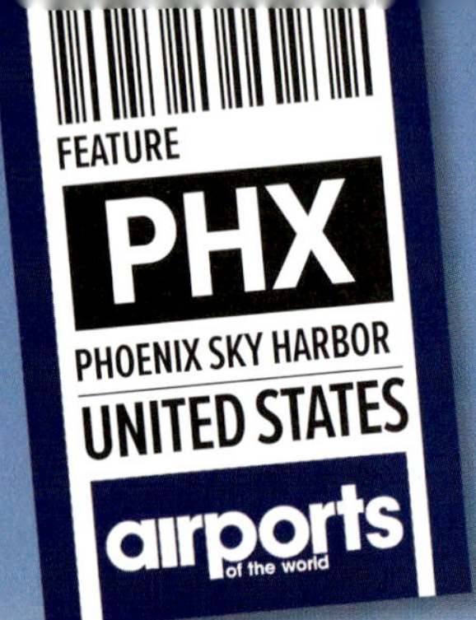

Soaring

In 2024, Phoenix Sky Harbor International Airport handled more than 50 million passengers in a single year for the first time ever. **Thomas Haynes** visited the American hub to find out what makes it tick

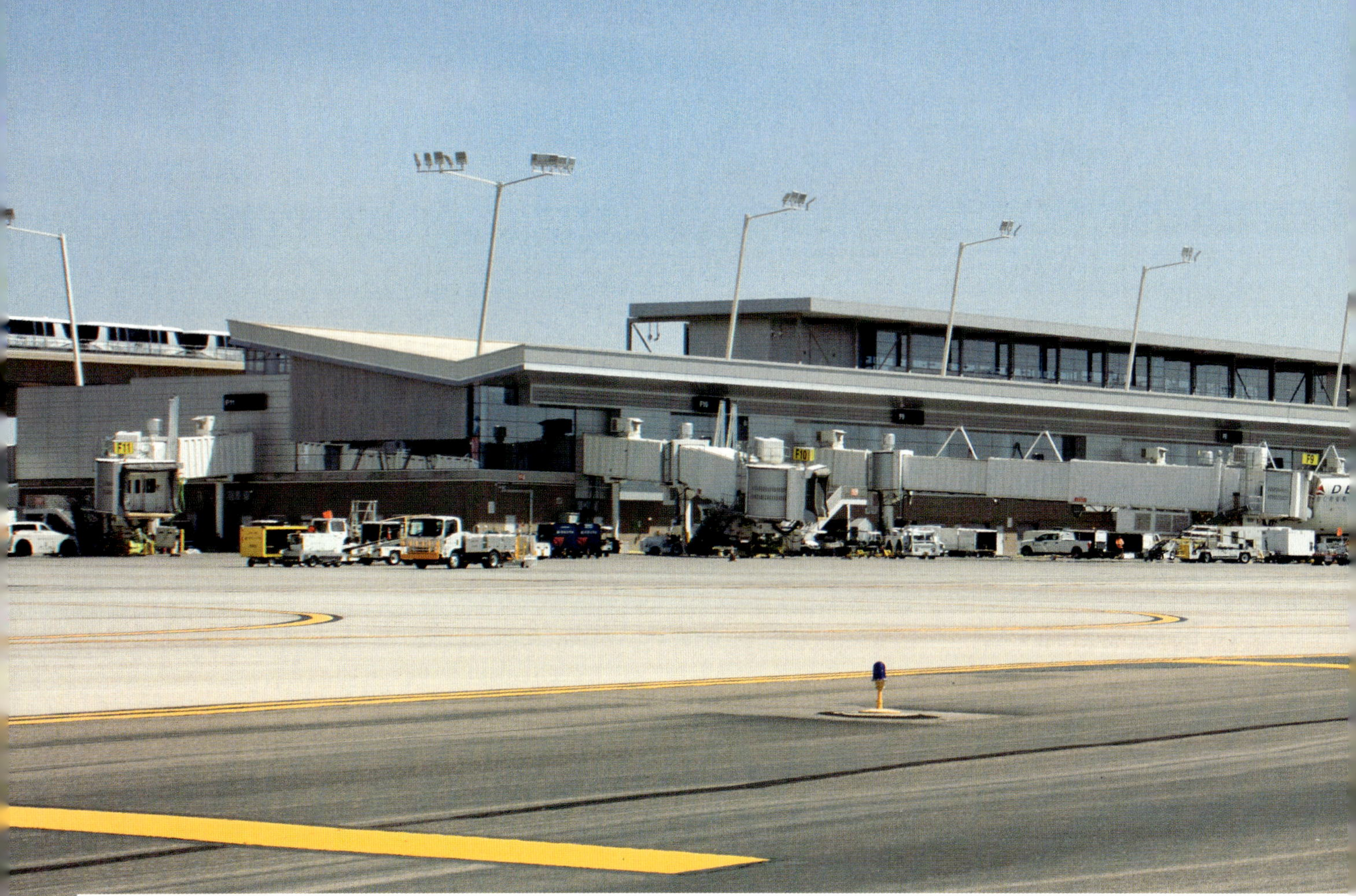

A view looking east across Phoenix Sky Harbor International Airport, with Terminal 3 in the foreground and Terminal 4 on the right *Key-Thomas Haynes*

Sky Harbor's record-setting passenger numbers of 2024 came ahead of a milestone year for the US facility which, in 2025, is celebrating 90 years since coming into public ownership when the City of Phoenix purchased the airport.

Situated around three miles east of downtown Phoenix, Sky Harbor is Arizona's largest and busiest airport, and is comfortably within the top 15 in the United States.

Setting up shop

It's nearly 100 years since the airport was established on the site it now occupies. In 1928, American aviation pioneer J Parker Van Zandt – who in 1927 setup Scenic Airways, which went on to become today's Grand Canyon Airlines – purchased 278 acres of farmland. The airline boss wanted to create a winter base for his airline's operations and thus settled on Phoenix to fulfil this role.

After a runway and hangar were constructed, the first scheduled passenger flights began from Sky Harbor in 1929 with Scenic Airways and its Ford Trimotor aircraft.

Not long after, owing to the Stock Market Crash of 1929, Van Zandt sold the airport to a consortium of local investors by the name of Acme Investments Company. This group owned the facility until 1935, when the City of Phoenix was persuaded to buy Sky Harbor for $100,000 – which is about $2.3m in today's money – a bargain really, when you consider the value of the investment today. The acquisition came about because American Airlines threatened to end its air service if the city did not take over the airport.

Flying activity at Sky Harbor picked up pace in the 1930s, with American operating a southern transcontinental

Sky Harbor

service between New York and Los Angeles. By 1939, the eight-stop service beginning at New York/Newark called at Washington, Nashville, Memphis, Dallas, Fort Worth, El Paso, Tucson, and Phoenix before arriving in LA at Glendale's Grand Central Air Terminal.

In November 1938, American was joined at Sky Harbor by Transcontinental and Western Air (TWA) which began both passenger and mail services between Phoenix and San Francisco. Later, other stops along the way included Boulder City, Las Vegas, Oakland and Fresno. By December 1940, airlines at the facility included American, TWA, Sky Harbor Air Service, and Southwest Airways, bringing the total number of aircraft based at Sky Harbor to 35.

Going for growth

As air traffic grew, so did the facilities. The first air traffic control tower was built in 1940, with a second storey being added four years later. Sky Harbor's first paved runway was added in 1945.

Total passenger traffic at the facility in 1950 was 240,786. In 1952, that number increased to 296,066. Subsequent years continued to see an increase in passenger traffic.

"I had no idea that it would be that busy," said Doug Carr, former assistant director of Sky Harbor in a past video interview. "During the years I was there (the late 1940s up until the mid-1950s), we always stayed close to number one, and occasionally we'd slip and go back to number two. I understand now that we're among the nation's busiest. It has just mushroomed. And it just kept growing and kept growing and it is still growing."

The expansion meant the need for a modern terminal, and as a result, Terminal 1 was constructed. It was built by Mardian Construction Company at a cost of

Airlines launched daily flights to Chicago and New York using the Boeing 720. Rival TWA followed suit in January 1961 with its Convair 880.

By 1962, Terminal 2 had been completed at a cost of $2.7m (approximately $28m in today's money). Covering 330,000sq ft and 19 gates, Terminal 2 was one of the United States' most modern facilities at the time. It was remodelled in 2007, with new shops and restaurants and an improved security checkpoint. With its opening, Phoenix planners hoped to service airline traffic until the year 2000, but passenger usage tripled again in less than a decade and building Terminal 3 became a necessity.

$835,000 (about $10m at today's prices) and completed in September 1952. One of its unique features was a new state-of-the-art 107ft tubular steel control tower with a 129-step spiral staircase. The terminal also featured an observation deck where aviation enthusiasts could watch the goings on.

As the 1950s came to a close, Sky Harbor unexpectedly entered the jet age with the arrival of an American Airlines Boeing 707. According to *The Arizona Republic* newspaper, the aircraft diverted to Sky Harbor because of bad weather in Los Angeles. Actress Marilyn Monroe was reportedly among the inconvenienced passengers.

In September 1960, jet service officially came to Sky Harbor when American

In 1967, Mrs Vern Cooper became the ten millionth airline passenger to depart from Sky Harbor since its official opening in 1928. She was presented with an orchid corsage by Mayor Milton Graham.

As 1970 rolled around, the US federal government designated Sky Harbor as an international port of entry and so the facility was renamed Phoenix Sky Harbor International Airport. Regular international operations began in 1971 with an Air West service to Guadalajara, Mexico.

This decade also saw Sky Harbor accept its first supersonic arrival. British Airways Concorde, G-BOAA (c/n 206), visited on December 12, 1978, for a training and promotional flight.

Construction of Terminal 3 began in 1976 and was completed in 1979 at a cost of $35m – today's equivalent of $154m. At the time, 4.4 million people were flying in and out of the airport annually. After its completion, passenger traffic grew to seven million. The facility offers 880,000sq ft of space and 23 gates on two concourses. By the end of 1985, passenger traffic rapidly increased to 11.6 million at Terminal 3.

America West Airlines became the first airline to officially call Sky Harbor its home when it began services in August 1983 using three leased Boeing 737-200s. The carrier quickly expanded and by the end of the following year boasted a 17-strong fleet. An October 1984 timetable showed nonstop services to 20 destinations and its first international service to Calgary via Las Vegas.

The airline became an increasingly dominant force at Sky Harbor as it grew and thus influenced the development of Terminal 4, construction of which began in October 1989. At a cost of $248m (approximately $608m today) – the building was the largest structural capital improvement project in Phoenix. Construction began on the terminal core and three concourses – two for use by America West and one for international arrivals – but prior to completion, a route expansion by Southwest Airlines required that it, too, be located in Terminal 4. Two more concourses were added, and the building opened in November 1990 with five concourses and 44 gates.

British Airways inaugurated a London/Gatwick connection on July 1, 1996, using one of its McDonnell Douglas ↘

DC-10s. According to *The Arizona Republic* newspaper, the airport hired a Beatles impersonation band and costumed bobbies [British police officers] to pose with passengers near the gate. Outside, the widebody was greeted by a water cannon salute as it taxied to the gate. In later years, the route was upgraded to the Boeing 747-400 and following the type's retirement, has been operated by the Airbus A350-1000. In 2002, Gatwick was swapped for London/Heathrow.

In 1998, a sixth concourse was added to Terminal 4, and the international concourse was expanded to include more gates. By March 2005, a seventh concourse providing eight extra gates had begun operation. In June 2022, another eight-gate concourse was added. Occupied by Southwest Airlines, the 275,000sq ft space has some unique features including 14,000sq ft of electrochromic glazing throughout the concourse. This intelligent technology provides various levels of tinting depending upon the level of sunlight at any given point during the day and not only helps to keep travellers comfortable, but also improves energy efficiency.

To facilitate international flights, arriving passengers are separated from departing passengers in Terminal 4, and its two-sided design allows for vehicle access from the east or west. Level 1, for arriving passengers, includes areas for baggage claim and ground transportation. Level 2, the departing passenger level, houses all ticket

PHX Sky Train

A notable feature of Sky Harbor is its automated people-mover system dubbed PHX Sky Train. Opening in 2013, after a series of extensions, the service now runs the full length of the airport and goes between Valley Metro Rail at 44th/ Washington Streets, the East Economy Parking area, the airport terminals, the 24th Street PHX Sky Train Station, and the Rental Car Center. It is free for travellers to use.

way for these developments. After nearly 40 years of operations, the 1952-built Terminal 1 was closed in 1990 and demolished the following year. Its location is now the site of the West Economy car park – ironically where the author parked on the day of his visit. After its remodelling in 2007, Terminal 2 continued in operation until February 2020 when it too was closed – it was demolished in 2021 with the space now home to concrete aircraft parking stands.

In 2025, the airport now has just two terminals with a combined total of 116 active aircraft gates. Terminal 3 offers 25 gates (ten in Concourse E and 15 in Concourse F) while Terminal 4 is the largest with 91 gates. It has eight

American Airlines is the largest carrier at Sky Harbor, boasting a 40% market share
Key-Thomas Haynes

counters. Food/beverage concessions, shops, and the entrances to all the concourses are on Level 3. Four levels of parking, some 3,400 spaces, top out the building. Terminal 4 currently has 92 gates.

Sky Harbor today

The airport has undergone what seems like constant development and improvement over the years. Its terminal facilities have been added to and upgraded as passenger traffic has grown.

It has also closed and demolished some of its older facilities to make

Unusually, Sky Harbor's fire trucks are painted red rather than the FAA-recommended green/yellow. This is because, unlike most US airports whose vehicles are federally funded, Sky Harbor purchased these trucks independently, and they also serve the local community from a fire station located on the airport's north side
Key-Thomas Haynes

Sky Harbor celebrated its 50th anniversary in 1985 with a series of balloons

Southwest Airlines is the second largest airline at Sky Harbor. In 2024, it handled 17.1 million customers representing a 32% share *Key-Thomas Haynes*

Chicago-based United Airlines carried 3.2 million passengers at Sky Harbor last year *Key-Thomas Haynes*

Denver-based Frontier Airlines was the fifth largest airline at Sky Harbor during 2024 when it carried more than 2.7 million passengers *Key-Thomas Haynes*

concourses split equally between north and south side of the building. There are 28 A gates divided equally between two concourses, and 31 B gates (divided into two concourses of 15 and 16). On the south side, four more concourses protrude, all offering eight gates each.

Sky Harbor boasts three runways dubbed north, centre and south, corresponding to their geographical location on the site. The former, designated 08/26, is the longest at 11,490ft. The centre runway, designated 07L/25R, is 10,300ft long, while the south runway, designated 07R/25L, is the shortest at 7,800ft long. All of the strips are 150ft wide.

Airlines galore

In 2025, the number of scheduled passenger airlines serving Sky Harbor totals 26. Terminal 3 is home to 15 of them including Advanced Airlines, Air Canada, Alaska Airlines, Allegiant Air, Breeze Airways, Delta Air Lines, Denver Air Connection, Frontier Airlines, Hawaiian Airlines, JetBlue Airways, Porter Airlines, Southern Airways Express, Spirit Airlines, Sun Country Airlines, and United Airlines. Terminal 4's airlines are Aeroméxico, Air France, American Airlines, British Airways, Contour Airlines, Flair Airlines, Southwest Airlines, Volaris and WestJet. Grand Canyon Airlines – whose founder also setup Sky Harbor –

maintains an operation at the Phoenix facility to this day. Based out of the Jackson Jet Center on the south side of the airport, the airline operates a double daily flight between Sky Harbor and Safford Airport, located some 140 miles to the southeast in Graham County.

Last year, Sky Harbor handled 52,325,266 passengers – the most in a single year in its history and the first time it has broken the 50 million mark. Approximately 75% of this traffic was served through Terminal 4, with the remaining 25% using Terminal 3.

According to the airport's statistics, the largest carrier at Sky Harbor last year was American Airlines which handled more than 21.1 million passengers – representing a 40% market share. The next largest was Southwest Airlines with 17.1 million customers – a 32% share. The next four carriers all handled in excess of one million people at Sky Harbor: Delta Air Lines (3.7 million), United Airlines (3.2 million), Frontier Airlines (2.7 million), and Alaska Airlines (1.5 million). British Airways – with its daily A350 link to Heathrow – carried

Terminal 4 with the glass Sky Train station in front and its distinctive car park spirals on each side *Key-Thomas Haynes*

just over 200,000 passengers to and from Sky Harbor during 2024.

Future development

With more than 50 million passengers last year and traveller numbers continuing to grow, a new terminal at Sky Harbor is in the long-term plan to enable the facility to meet passenger demand.

In May 2024, the airport confirmed a plan to build a new facility at the western end of the airport campus near where the former Terminals 1 and 2 were located. Work on the terminal design is still ongoing. Planning and environmental preparation will take several years, and construction is not anticipated to begin until after 2030. The airport says the project will be funded with passenger facility charges, bonds, and airport funding with no tax dollars to be used.

"Phoenix Sky Harbor is busier than ever, which is why we'll soon need a new terminal to accommodate our growth," said the city's mayor Kate Gallego. "To continue providing excellent customer experience, the council and I are moving forward with plans to build a cutting-edge terminal at the airport's west end. The new expansion is years in the making and I am looking forward to the continued work to turn our shared vision into reality."

In the nearer term, work began in April 2025 on a new $326m concourse in Terminal 3, which will add six extra gates to the facility. Dubbed North 2, the structure will add approximately 173,000sq ft of space across a multi-level design. The new elevated connector bridge will link the North 2 Concourse to the existing Terminal 3 structure, and the design also includes provisions for a future tunnel connection to Terminal 4's North Concourse. Moving walkways and lifts will be strategically placed to ensure ease of access between the various levels, optimising passenger flow throughout the expanded terminal.

Elsewhere in the plan, the airport wants to improve airfield efficiency with a new north/south taxiway on the western side of the airport. This will involve moving the cargo operation to the east. An expansion to the centre runway is also on the cards to "satisfy the increased need for a longer departure runway". ✈

Above: **Low-cost carrier Spirit Airlines uses Terminal 3 at Sky Harbor**
Key-Thomas Haynes

Left: **Delta Air Lines Boeing 757-232, N6713Y (c/n 30777), rolls out on runway 08 after a three-and-a-half-hour flight from Atlanta**
Key-Thomas Haynes

KANSAI
THE SENSEI

As the world's first airport built on an artificial island, Kansai taught the industry valuable lessons. To mark its 30th anniversary, **Robert Veitch** looks back at the life and times of this Japanese game–changer

Sixty one years ago, back in 1964, the first jet aircraft began arriving at Osaka/Itami, which initiated noise complaints from nearby residents. Located in the dense residential suburbs of northern Osaka, the airport had no capacity for runway expansion and the single terminal was becoming increasingly crowded. The search for a replacement began in earnest.

By April 1968, the Japanese Ministry of Transport (JMOT) had begun surveying eight proposed sites. Avoiding noise pollution and urban areas were key priorities. Almost six years later, the Japanese Council for Civil Aviation submitted a report to the JMOT recommending an off shore area in Osaka Bay. Further preparatory work took place and, by May 1981, dialogue with local communities was underway. The Japanese minister of transport

asked Osaka prefectural governors to co-operate in the construction of the new airport and, in July 1982, they gave their consent to implement the plan. In October 1984, Kansai International Airport Company (KIAC) was founded and a proposal to create an airport in the bay was approved.

Building off shore offered the tantalising possibility of 24-hour operations and the potential for seamless expansion in the decades that followed. Developing a pioneering facility would also help revitalise western Japan, which had been losing ground to Tokyo as the 20th Century progressed. In choosing Osaka Bay, the airport would become the world's first to be built on an artificial island.

The island
Water depth at the site was approximately 60ft and the band of clay

beneath the seabed was 66ft thick and highly permeable – up to 70% water. Settlement occurs naturally with the addition of weight from above, but to speed up the process, a 5ft thick sand blanket was deposited on the seabed, before sand drains were used to reduce the water content in the clay.

A million of these 65ft long, 16in diameter sand drains were injected into the seabed at 2.5m intervals, each forcing water from the clay. Sand drains had first been used in Japan in 1952, but Kansai needed more than the previous 35 years combined. Water cannot be squeezed from clay as fast as from a sponge, so ever-decreasing settlement was expected to continue after the airport was opened, until land consolidation had finally taken place.

During January 1987, construction of the 6.8 mile perimeter seawall started – the visible section above the waterline

The exterior of the central section of Terminal 1 at dusk
Renzo Piano Building Workshop/ Hata Yoshio

included 48,000 wave-dissipating concrete tetrapods. During June, the installation of piers for the bridge to the mainland began. Concurrently, a competition to design the airport took place. It was won the following year with an innovative creation from Italy's Renzo Piano Building Workshop, who had designed the Pompidou Centre in Paris and would later build The Shard in London.

By the end of the 1980s, the seawall was complete and land reclamation was underway. Three mountains were excavated to provide the rock, which was shipped by 80 barges a day and deposited on the sea floor from 4am-11pm. By December 1991, after 180 million cubic metres of rock (equivalent to approximately 70,000 Olympic swimming pools) and ten million man hours, the 1,260 acre island, measuring 2.5 miles long and 1.6 miles wide, was complete.

From the ground up

Construction of the airport began in May 1991 and, by the end of December 1993, the runways, taxiways and aprons were complete. What would become runway 06R/24L measured 11,463ft long and 197ft wide. In March 1994, seven years after it was started, The Sky Gate Bridge R (Kansai International Airport Access Bridge), the world's longest double-decker truss bridge, was completed. At 2.33 miles long, 97ft wide and 82ft high at the highest point above the water, it carries six lanes of traffic on the upper deck and two railway lines on the lower deck. That June, Kansai Airport Station was opened, creating the first scheduled links with the mainland, with the rapid transit to Namba station in central Osaka taking around 45 minutes. Kansai is also linked to Kobe Airport by a 30-minute ferry service.

Renzo Piano's cutting-edge, four-storey terminal building came to symbolise the world's first airport built on a man-made island. Seen from above it resembles a glider: a fuselage and tailplane with two elegant wings stretching out across the firmament. At 1.1 miles it is the longest terminal on earth, 206ft longer than Concourse A, McNamara Terminal at Detroit/Metropolitan. It was built with 42 boarding gates, to accommodate up to 100,000 passengers a day and designed to withstand earthquakes and typhoons.

The commission requested unobstructed aircraft visibility from the departure level of the terminal. Piano's asymmetrical design incorporated an aerofoil-shaped, clear-span roof with glazed facades facing the runway and opaque surfaces sweeping in the opposite direction. The height of the wings decreases towards the terminal extremities, following a gentle curve, to ensure the 262ft-high control tower's line of vision across the island remains unobstructed. The roof aids air circulation because air flows across the underside from the rear to the glazed facades, which means air conditioning ducts suspended from the ceiling were not required. As a result, ceiling sculptures in the check-in zone are in continuous movement.

Because of its length, the Wing Shuttle was built to make movement within the terminal easier. Two pairs of automated people movers transport passengers from the central section to the extremities of both wings, 2,220ft away, via a midway station. It is the only airport people mover in Japan.

On September 4, 1994, Kansai International Airport was opened, instantly becoming the largest gateway into western Japan. Overnight, ground support equipment was moved from Itami, which then regressed from an international to a regional facility, after plans to close it were met with complaints from nearby residents on economic grounds.

Island II

Though newly open, the addition of freight flights saw the airport at its limit during peak periods, so expansion plans were hatched and, in April 1998, work on a second island began. Slightly larger than its sibling at 1,347 acres, it required 1.2 million sand drains and 250 million cubic metres of rock, equivalent to approximately 1.5 billion bathtubs. In October 2005, construction of the second runway started and, on August 2, 2007, it opened as 06L/24R, some 13,123ft long and 197ft wide. Within a month, Kansai became a 24-hour facility.

Above: The 6.8 mile perimeter seawall includes 48,000 wave dissipating concrete tetrapods
Vinci Airports

Above middle: Land reclamation required 180 million cubic metres of rock, supplied by 80 barges a day, operating from 4am-11pm, which began in early 1990
Kansai Airports

Right: The sky museum is home to a 98ft model of Kansai's Terminal 1
Kansai Airports

Construction of Terminal 2 began in October 2011 and it would become the first dedicated low-cost terminal in Japan. Domestic operations commenced on October 28, 2012, with international services beginning in January 2017, after the terminal had been expanded. It has 22 gates, split into separate domestic and international sectors. A single-storey building without airbridges – passengers are lent umbrellas for their walk to the aircraft when it rains – a far cry from its glamourous sibling on the other island.

The two terminals are connected by free shuttle buses, or else passengers can walk the 1.25 miles through KIX Sora Park and Waterside Green Park.

Subsidence and storms

The first island was expected to settle by 18ft as it compressed the seabed, yet it sank 27ft within the first five years – almost twice the expected rate. In conversation with *Airports of the World*, Kenji Takanishi, from the group corporate communications department at Kansai, said: "The amount of settlement now varies from place to place, and different settlement levels cause problems such as distortion of the structure." Engineers installed steel plates beneath the 906 hydraulic jacks (latterly increased) on which the columns of Terminal 1 rest, which are adjusted to keep it level. Settlement continues at an ever-decreasing rate – 7cm annually by 2008, down to 6cm annually since 2015. Kansai has sunk a total of 38ft, but is expected to stabilise at 13ft above sea level. For comparison, the city of Venice averages 3ft above sea level.

Terminal 1 emerged unscathed from its first natural test: the Hanshin (Kobe) earthquake on January 17, 1995, a 7.3 magnitude event on the Richter scale with its epicentre around 15 miles away. Kansai also survived a typhoon with winds speeds exceeding 130mph in September 1998, but Typhoon Jebi in 2018 would provide a tougher test...

Japan's most powerful storm since 1993, Jebi struck on September 4. Storm surges rendered large parts of the airport inoperable and some aircraft were marooned in water up to engine level. A drifting ocean tanker hit and damaged the bridge, severing the link to the mainland. Around 3,000 passengers were stranded overnight, without power, before ferries and speedboats evacuated them. The airport was closed for two days, but rail services resumed on ⤵

Below left: **Gates 19-23 at Terminal 1** *Kansai Airports*

Below: **The impressive check-in roof at Terminal 1** *Renzo Piano Building Workshop/ Ishida Shunji*

Renovations to the international departures area were opened in December 2023 *Vinci Airports*

September 18, and the airport was back to full capacity on September 21.

Operations

Once open, Kansai charged the highest landing fees on the planet. Construction costs had been high and the Japanese government was pressed to bear a higher burden of the cost to keep the airport attractive to airlines and passengers. As the millennium passed, the facility processed its first 100 million passengers. Five years later, that number had doubled.

Terminal 1 was updated between 2012 and 2015. Further improvements began in 2021 and, by 2022, an enhanced domestic area was unveiled, followed at the end of 2023 by revisions to the international departures and passport control area. Work continued until March 2025, when the revamped security checkpoint became operational.

Right: The Terminal 1 check-in hall showing ceiling sculptures in continuous movement *Renzo Piano Building Workshop/ Shingu Susumu*

Below: The height of the wings decreases towards the terminal extremities to ensure the control tower's line of vision across the entire island *Kansai Airports*

> Kansai is a hub for All Nippon Airways (ANA), Japan Airlines and low-cost carrier Peach, and is used by more than 65 other operators flying to over 100 destinations

As Takanishi noted: "In autumn 2026, the north-south commercial facilities in the international departure area will be expanded. We will continue to constantly review the airport with new ideas and lead Japan in terms of comfort, convenience and operations."

Today, Kansai is a hub for All Nippon Airways (ANA), Japan Airlines and low-cost carrier Peach, and is used by more than 65 other operators flying to over 100 destinations. Since 2014, FedEx has operated its North Pacific Regional Hub at the site, one of more than 20 cargo carriers to use the airport. Passenger numbers peaked in 2019 at 31,915,607 when Kansai was the third busiest airport in Japan. The COVID-19 pandemic saw numbers plummet to three million in 2021, but year-on-year uplifts have followed. Terminal 1 has capacity for 25 million passengers annually and Terminal 2 for 8.35 million. Once developments at the former are complete, airport capacity will increase to 40 million passengers.

Takanishi confirmed there are no plans for a third island and runway, but rail connectivity may be improved: "The Naniwa-suji Line, which will improve access between Shin-Osaka Station, where the Shinkansen bullet train stops, and Kansai, is scheduled for spring 2031."

One astonishing record the airport holds is that there has never been a recorded item of lost baggage, an almost incomprehensible level of perfection.

All Nippon Airways Boeing 737-881, JA65AN (c/n 33903), starting its departure rollout while Jetstar Japan Airbus A320-232, JA10JJ (c/n 5520), awaits its turn *Key Collection*

Lessons for the future

Kansai became the most expensive civil engineering project in Japanese history at £7.3bn, with another £300m spent since completion. Yet the expertise gained and lessons learned were applied to projects at Hong Kong (1998), Chubu Centrair (2005), Kobe (2006) and Kitakyushu (2006). On April 19, 2001, the American Society of Civil Engineers awarded Kansai one of its ten Monuments of the Millennium awards in the Airport Design and Development category.

Takanishi concluded: "The aim was to create an airport that would not pollute Osaka Bay and would be friendly to the natural environment. Since the beginning of construction, efforts have been made to harmonise man-made structures with nature and these efforts continue to this day. The airport is the gateway to the Kansai region, and we believe it plays a very important role in the development of the economy."

An island airport with potentially limitless opportunity for expansion, an innovative earthquake proof clear-span terminal on hydraulic jacks with duct-free air conditioning, uninterrupted views of the apron, automated in-terminal people movers, fuels of the future, Kansai has proved to be a game-changer and a teacher to those that have paddled offshore in its pioneering wake.

Spotter's heaven

At the northeast corner of the first island, Kansai offers spotters the chance to take photographs from open air, 360° panoramic sky deck on the fifth floor. Two floors below, the sky museum has hands-on exhibits, including a 98ft model of Terminal 1. The sky shop is the self-styled 'best place in Japan' for airline- and airport-related goods. Airport tours lasting 90-minutes also operate from this building.

Acknowledgements

Thanks to Momoka Wakabayashi at Kansai Airports and Stefania Canta at Renzo Piano Building Workshop for their help with this article

The fifth floor of the open air, 360° panoramic sky deck offers excellent spotting opportunities for aviation enthusiasts *Key Collection*

FEATURE
DWC
DUBAI
UNITED ARAB EMIRATES
airports of the world

DUBAI *dream*

The government in Dubai has approved plans for a $32bn mega-hub at Al Maktoum. **Richard Schuurman** takes a look at what could become the largest airport in the world

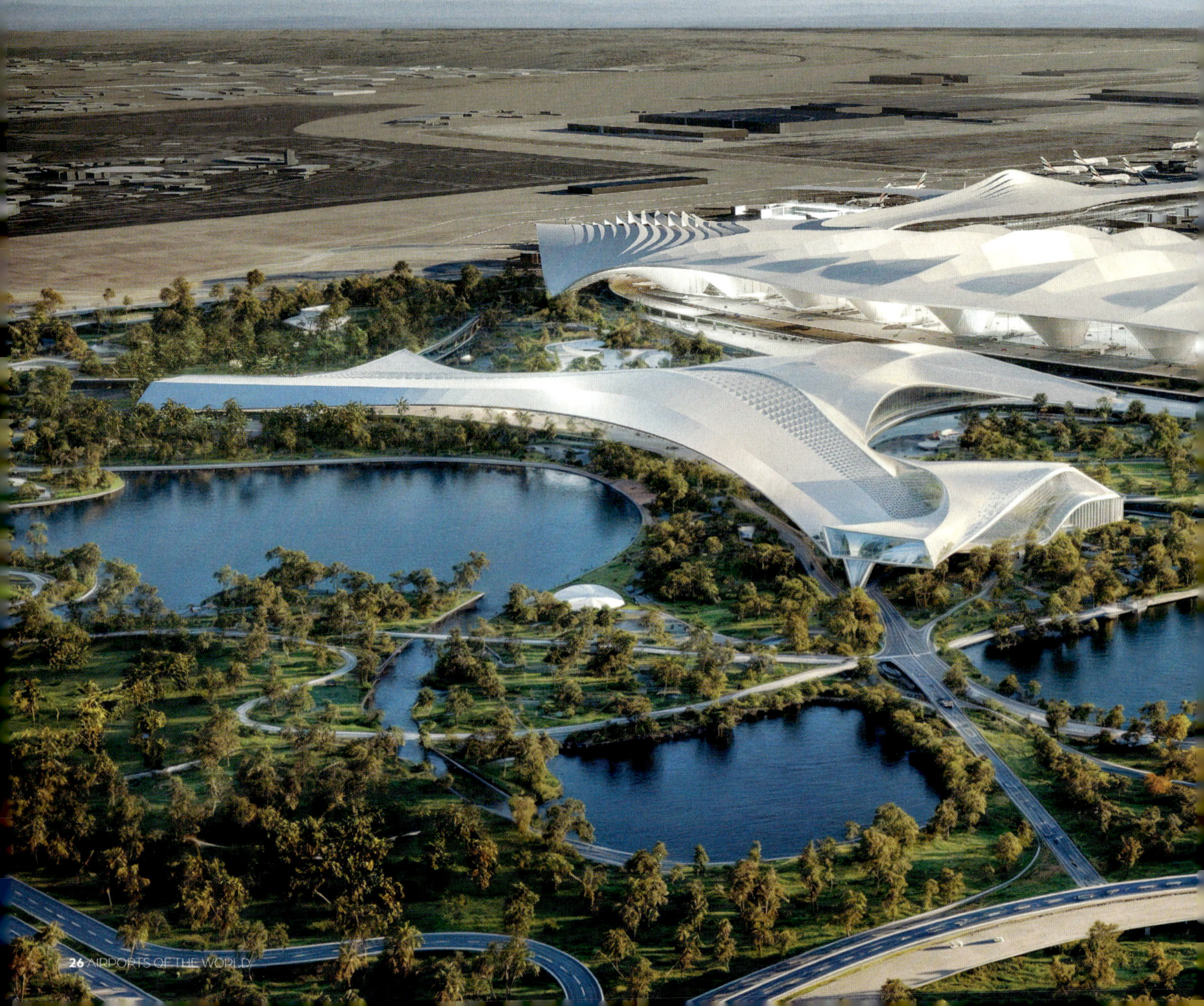

t won't be long before ground excavators and thousands of workers arrive at a 70km² area in Dubai South and start building the world's biggest airport. In April 2024, some five years after plans were put on hold, the city's ruler, Sheikh Mohammed bin Rashid Al Maktoum, approved the designs for the $32bn investment in the new Dubai/Al Maktoum International Airport. Within ten years, phase one, with a capacity for 150 million annual passengers must be operational. Eventually, the hub will be expanded to a capacity of 260 million annual passengers and have 400 aircraft stands.

Al Maktoum is an existing airport that's a 90-minute drive from downtown Dubai. It opened for cargo operations in June 2010 and welcomed its first passenger flights in October 2013. An extension in 2018 increased capacity to 26 million passengers annually, but real-world traffic has never got close to this and the 1.6 million passengers that passed through in 2019 remains the highest number the current terminal has processed. In 2024, just 540,000 people used Al Maktoum in comparison to the 87 million that passed through Dubai/International.

In September 2014, Sheikh Mohammed and the Dubai government approved ⬊

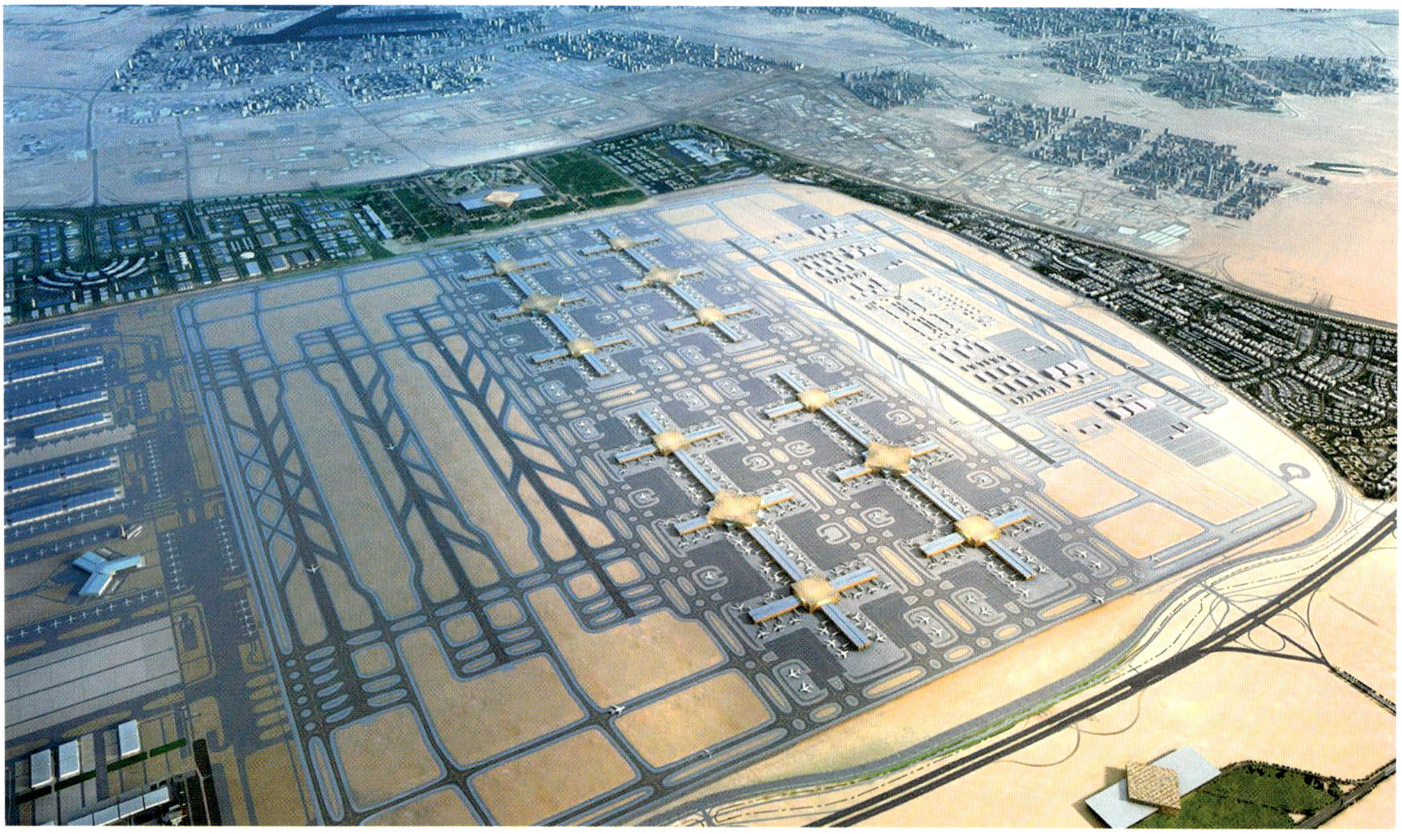

Above: **The original design for Al Maktoum had a gate-free terminal and four long concourses, each with three nodes and gates**

Right: **Adel Al Redha, deputy president and COO at Emirates** *Emirates*

Below: **The Dubai/International terminal in the 1960s, with an Iran Air DC-3 in attendance**

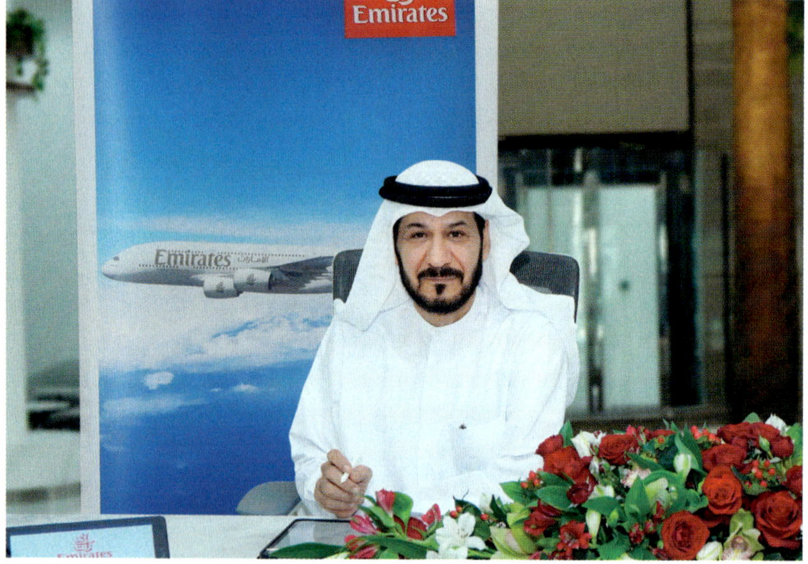

the development of phase two at Al Maktoum. The plan then was for 220-240 million annual passengers and a 2025 opening. Groundbreaking did start in 2016 on the first of five planned runways, but the project was put on hold in 2018-2019. Five years later, it received the second go-ahead.

On the sidelines of the International Air Transport Association (IATA) AGM in Dubai in early June 2024, *Airliner World* magazine discussed the 2024-2034 expansion plan with Paul Griffiths, CEO of Dubai Airports, and Adel Al Redha, deputy president and chief operating officer of Emirates.

Pause for thought

Griffiths revealed the reason behind the pausing of phase one in 2018-2019: “The principal reason has been

“The aim is to have a no-red-lights policy, where people simply pass through the airport at the speed that they want”

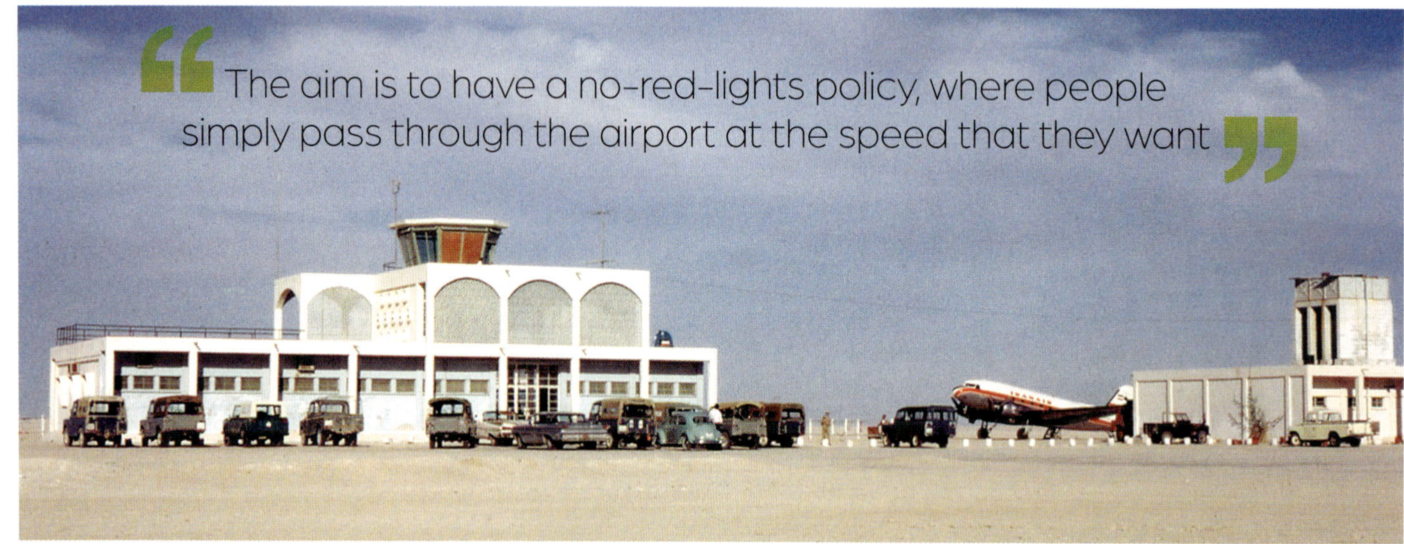

that technology at airports has been improving all the time. We were finding that we were able to accommodate the growth of all the airline customers at [Dubai/International] through the introduction of new technology, because for the same infrastructure, if you are able to double the flow rate that technology enables, you effectively double the capacity without building anything."

With technology facilitating increased passenger numbers at Dubai/International, it was expected to handle 91 million passengers in 2024. As Griffiths noted: "We think that 120 million is about the limit. When I first arrived [in 2007], the limit was 65 million. So we constantly found ways to increase that through technology and infrastructure. We've opened three new concourses and a new terminal since 2008. However, that strategy can only last for so long. So the government decided that it wanted to allocate the $32bn necessary to build the new airport and give it sufficient time for it to be developed. I think it is a very good strategic move because, ultimately, it will allow us to go beyond the runway movement rate and the stand numbers that we have at DXB, which are the ultimate constraints."

A fresh look

The decision to restart the project came after a thorough rethink, which resulted in significant changes. What's unchanged is that Al Maktoum will have five runways: three to the south of the concourses (including the existing strip), one to the north and a fifth positioned further to the north, separated by MRO and cargo facilities. Four will be operational, with the fifth on standby. The MRO complex includes new hangars commissioned by Emirates and flydubai in November 2023.

Following the rethink, the terminal concept has drastically changed. The previous design had a gate-free terminal to the west, plus four long concourses, each with three nodes and gates. In the new design, the western terminal is enlarged, U-shaped and covered in a vast white canopy, with gates

Al Maktoum is being designed to handle 260 million passengers a year

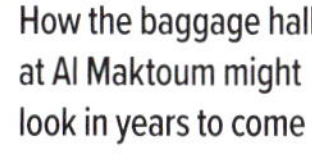

How the baggage hall at Al Maktoum might look in years to come

Left: Could this be the future entrance to the world's biggest airport?

Below: An artist's impression of how the main terminal building may look in 2032-2033

Top: Inside the current terminal at Al Maktoum

Above: The A380, so ubiquitous at Dubai/ International, will be in her final years when Al Maktoum opens *Emirates*

Right: An artist's impression of the new terminal exterior

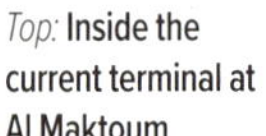

The existing terminal at Al Maktoum was built with the capacity for 26 million passengers annually, but has never exceeded 1.6 million

extending from the 'arms' of the huge building, while four smaller concourses will each have two nodes. Griffiths noted: "These are very much artists' impressions. There is a huge amount of modelling to be done. We have got a lot of proving of new techniques to do, because if we just end up designing a 20th Century airport for the 21st Century, we won't have achieved any of our objectives."

Al Redha added: "The concept of what the building will look like has been finalised by the government. We are working closely now with Dubai Aviation Engineering Projects in defining our future requirements for the forecasted number of passenger movements, the number of gates, lounges and check-in desks, as well as what other airlines want."

Ease of movement

Predicting how a 2030s or 2040s airport should look is no mean feat, but both Griffiths and Al Redha say the focus for Al Maktoum is on two major elements: passenger processing and ground connectivity. Griffith said: "We have to try and pre-empt the changes that are going to happen in both service technology and airport processes and design the most ideal airport. First of all, we hope that there won't be any physical stops. It will all be biometrics or a similar technology. The idea is that everyone will only stop when they want to stop. So if they want

> At 260 million passengers and five times the size of Dubai/International, the new Al Maktoum is set to raise the bar

The current terminal exterior at Al Maktoum Airport

have a drink, a meal or buy something, that will be at their discretion, but the aim is to have a no-red-lights policy, where people just simply pass through the airport at the speed they want. We won't have check-in, in my view, there will just be a very simple way of dropping a bag. Security, immigration, all of those things will be seamless and invisible and that will make for a far better passenger experience."

Al Redha added: "Your journey through the airport will become seamless thanks to biometric machines and cameras. Before, it was facial recognition with the eyes, now it is any point of the face. The accuracy of determining someone's identity is more accurate than maybe three years ago. But the principle remains the same: you should have a free path as you go through the airport. Over the next years, the implementation of such principles will be more accurate, cheaper and advanced, but it remains the same."

It's logical that the new airport design is more compact, as Griffiths revealed: "One thing that we are working on very diligently is the elimination of the vast walking distances that are often associated with modern airports. Rather than having a walking distance to a common channel for security and immigration, if we can have many different channels, each of fairly low capacity, then you can take a customer on their chosen mode of surface transport, very close to their airplane. So each of the concourses in our design will have their point of entry from their external environments. The design of that interface between the surface transport and the airport infrastructure is incredibly important."

Griffiths elaborated: "The idea is that the surface interface will not be just one area, it will be in many different areas – really going back to the old model in airports like London/Heathrow that used to have the Oceanic and Britannic terminals: you go to a place which is connected to the other terminals, but which is specific to the destination you are going to. That means it is more of an intimate experience and you can get closer to your airplane. All of the retail and lounge facilities will be close to where your departure point will be. It will be a wholly different and hopefully much better experience for our customers. The idea is to take you closer to your point of destination, not drop you off in the middle and then expect you to walk one or two kilometres to your aircraft."

No A380s

For Emirates, operations at Al Maktoum in 2040 will differ significantly from those today at Dubai/International. By then, the Airbus A380s will be coming to the end of their 30-year career. The Boeing 777-9 will become the carrier's biggest aircraft, supported by 777-8s, A350s, 787s and whatever airframes may come along between now and then. The retirement of the A380s will affect the airline and the airport, as Al Redha explained: "For sure, the end of the A380 is taken into account. They are Code F planes with a bigger span. When they are gone, you have more space to slot in more airplanes. That is being defined when it comes to the number of gates."

Griffiths expects narrowbodies to become more prominent at the new airport: "The range capability of narrowbody aircraft is now very significant. Of the 14,000+ aircraft currently on order books with manufacturers, only 15% are widebodies. So the distinction between widebody and narrowbody aircraft is becoming more and more blurred. The number of city pairs you are able to fly to from [Al Maktoum] will increase dramatically and the frequency you will be able to enjoy to those city pairs will also increase. I am anticipating a huge increase in the number of movements and a decrease in the average aircraft size."

	Dubai/International	Dubai/Al Maktoum
IATA code	DXB	DWC
Opened	1963	2010
Land area	7,200 acres	36,000 acres
Runways	2	5
Passengers in 2023	86,878,000	540,000
Max passenger capacity	120 million	260 million

Above: **Dubai/International in the 1970s**

TOpo right: **Paul Griffiths, CEO of Dubai Airports** *IATA*

Above right: **Al Maktoum hopes that its airport security will eventually become seamless and invisible**

Below: **Flydubai is the second largest operator at the UAE capital** *Flydubai*

Location, location, location

Although it's some way from many of Dubai's key attractions, Griffiths thinks the location of the new airport is a no-brainer: "Actually, the only way the city is to expand is obviously away from the border with Sharjah, to the south. The big change will be in surface transport — expect to see fast rail, an extension of the metro, better roads. In fact, by the time [Al Maktoum] really starts to approach capacity, we will see a whole new surface transport environment. Unmanned aerial vehicles, driverless cars, all sorts of different technologies will take us to the airport. By then, I am sure, every Dubai resident will be able to get to [Al Maktoum] as fast as they can get to [Dubai/International] today."

At 260 million passengers, and five times the size of Dubai/International the new Al Maktoum is set to raise the bar. With significant airport capacity in this part of the Middle East at Abu Dhabi and Qatar, and with Saudi Arabia planning major hubs in Riyadh and Jeddah, could Al Maktoum be too big? Not so, thinks Griffiths: "The plan is very real because if you look at the growth of Dubai and the growth of the city, they have gone hand-in-hand. When I arrived 17 years ago, we had 30 million passengers; this year, we are going to have 91 million passengers. So in ten years' time, you could be forgiven for thinking that perhaps we are actually not thinking big enough, because of the ongoing growth of Dubai and the success of the city suggests that an airport of that size is actually required. It is not a pie-in-the-sky project."

For Emirates, moving home will present operational challenges according to Al Redha: "As the government said, it will be open within ten years, so that is by 2032-2033 for the initial phase. We start with the main terminal and the nodes come later." Although Emirates president Sir Tim Clark said movement to the new airport will be done quickly, Al Redha took a slightly different view: "Once the airport is open, we will transfer flights, but I don't think it will be overnight. If you look at the operations at [Dubai/International], it will be a gradual movement of not just Emirates, but also other airlines like flydubai. It has to be well-planned and synchronised."

As for the current Al Maktoum terminal, Griffiths said it will operate as a standalone facility: "I am sure, we will find an airline or airlines that will want to use it as a very effective terminal. Passengers do like it very much. Those without the need to connect to the main terminal will find it a very efficient hub for them." Once Al Maktoum is fully operational, Dubai/International will cease to exist and the area will be redeveloped for an as yet undecided purpose.

> ❝ The number of city pairs you are able to fly to from Al Maktoum will increase dramatically and the frequency will also increase ❞

The World's Fastest Growing Aviation Website

Join us online

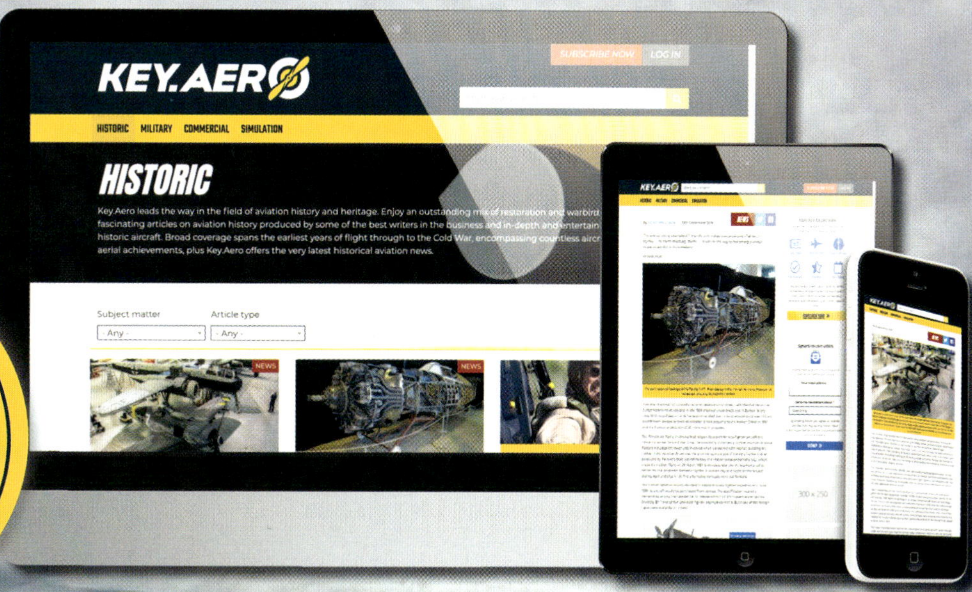

> "In-depth content and high-quality photography"
> **Stew**

> "Well worth the money"
> **Andy**

> "A great place for aviation geeks!"
> **Kenneth**

GREAT REASONS TO SUBSCRIBE

- In-depth articles, videos, quizzes and more, with new material added daily

- From historic and military aviation to commercial and simulation – *Key.Aero* has it all

- Exclusive interactive content you won't find anywhere else

- A fully searchable archive

- Access to all the leading aviation magazines

- Membership to an engaged, global aviation community

- Access on any device – anywhere, anytime

www.key.aero

Subscribe FROM JUST £5.99 for unlimited access

Inseparable
friends

FEATURE
LEQ
LAND'S END
UNITED KINGDOM
airports of the world

FEATURE
ISC
ST MARY'S
UNITED KINGDOM
airports of the world

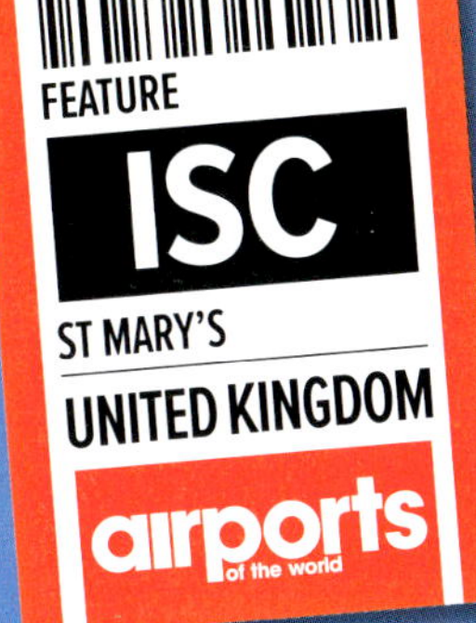

Robert Veitch travels from Land's End to St Mary's on the Isles of Scilly to discover how their airports work in symbiosis to connect remote communities

Aviation articles rarely start in railways stations, yet when contemplating a trip to the Scilly Isles and within range of London Paddington station, it's worth considering the 'Night Riviera'. Like a long-haul flight, a long-distance train offers a tangible sense of journey, but the sleeper train is something else... like the ultra-long-haul flight.

Diesel engines on the behemoth rumble into life a minute or two before the 11.45pm departure from platform one. After the smallest of jolts, the bronze of Paddington Bear starts to fade from view. Sleep comes and goes with the clickety-clack of the tracks, amplified by a comforting sense of sleep-inducing movement in the darkness. Breakfast is served by 7am and outside the urban vistas are long gone, replaced by the rolling Cornish landscape. At the end of the line in Penzance, the pre-booked airport transfer is waiting outside the station. After six miles and 20 minutes, just beyond the brow of a hill, Land's End Airport sits at the end of the road.

Life at the frontier

With a wooden exterior and slate roof, the only clue to what's inside is the air traffic control (ATC) tower protruding into the sky. Inside, the step-free terminal manages to achieve the incongruous feat of being spacious yet compact. Glulam beams and vaulted ceilings assert a homely feeling, enhanced by the log burner, laminate wood flooring, art installations, wall-mounted photos, giant lampshades, and plenty of seating. Beyond the floor to ceiling windows aircraft sit on the apron, and in the distance, the shadows of the Scillies are hazy ripples on the horizon. At the far end of the terminal, beyond Western Rocks café, which champions homemade and Cornish produce, is the exterior terrace where the smell of aviation fuel, and the thrill of aircraft firing up their propellors can be experienced at close quarters.

Chris Pearson is airport manager and senior ATC officer at Land's End. He told me: "I came here straight from the College of Air Traffic Control in Bournemouth. I did my first shift in September 1997 so I've climbed up the old and new tower many times." He explained that Land's End has a slightly larger facility than its counterpart across the water. "We're not as limited, but we can't take a loaded Dash 8 – we had the British Antarctic Survey Dash 7 land empty. They're from the same family as the Twin Otters, and that Dash 7 on runway 34 is probably the biggest thing we've had. We've had Pilatus PC-12 turboprops operating into the airfield as well."

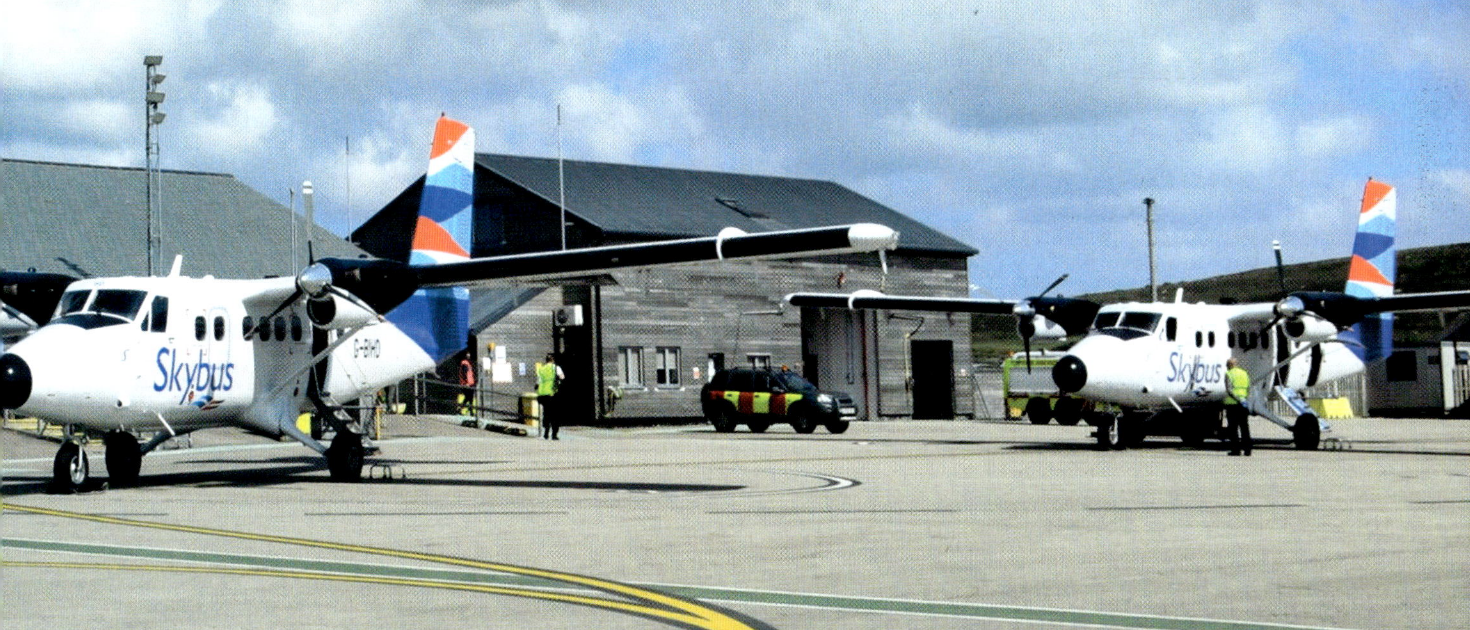

Land's End history

An airfield has existed here since 1935 with flights to the Scillies commencing on September 13, 1937, when a Channel Air Ferries de Havilland DH.84 Dragon, G-ADCR (c/n 6094), from Land's End touched down on St Mary's golf course. Channel Air Ferries became Great Western and Southern Airlines, introducing de Havilland DH.89 Dragon Rapides during World War Two, and was then taken over by British European Airways in 1947. Competition arrived in 1965, in the form of Scillonia Airways, but they were gone by 1969, the same year that Elizabeth Taylor opened a new terminal building. Westward Airways opened in 1970 and operated a flying school from 1971 to 2009.

The Isles of Scilly Skybus began scheduled services in August 1984 and remains the facility's primary operator. Its owner, The Isles of Scilly Steamship Group, purchased the airport in January 2012. The current terminal, built on the footprint of Westward Airways' flying school, opened on April 9, 2013, having cost £975,000. Where its 1969 predecessor had the words 'Lands End' painted in large white capital letters across the corrugated roof, the new iteration has solar panels.

The lingering after-effects of COVID-19 created a unique scenario in April 2021 when the Land's End – St Mary's route was named the UK's busiest that month. Skybus operated 363 flights, flying more than 3,100 passengers and was busier than LHR-JFK. The staycation boom that followed in 2021 saw Land's End experience its busiest July ever, with more than 8,500 passengers passing through its doors, of which 1,541 were day trips to the Scillies.

Like a long-haul flight, a long-distance train offers a tangible sense of journey

and regulations, including a 30-minute break every two hours. One important feature in the tower is the flight strip board, which consists of hand-written, colour-coded paper strips representing flights, which are moved around the board to show exactly what is happening in the airspace around the airport. Pearson explained: "Anything above 4,000ft tends to go to a radar service, Culdrose or Newquay, the two nearest units. We also work traffic up to 8,000ft on occasions, 10,000ft is our actual radio limit. On a busy day in July and August, there can be up to 120 movements a day."

After all these years he remains enthusiastic about his work: "It's unique. You get to know everybody; pilots, engineers, air traffic control, fire crew – and you wouldn't get that in a big airport because you're very separate departments. I just love the smell and busyness; there's always a buzz."

The Land's End terminal manages to achieve the incongruous feat of being spacious yet compact

Pearson was clear – the focus remains on the core offering: "We are a niche airport that serves the Isles of Scilly, that's our primary purpose. We also work with Flynqy Pilot Training in Newquay, and the Air Cornwall flying school who use an Ikarus C42 aircraft. Trinity House is based here and we get the Cornwall Air Ambulance and the Coastguard search and rescue Sikorsky S-92, and we provide a service to [Starspeed] helicopters every time they pass Penzance. I think we're the 37th busiest airport in the UK, which is amazing."

Being at the western end of the Cornish peninsula is advantageous for flights to the Scillies but detrimental in other ways: "I think you would struggle to fill the aircraft from here to [Exeter and Newquay]. We used to offer Exeter Christmas shopping flights, but it's the amount of time it ties the aircraft up for. For example, Southampton is getting on for two hours out, two hours back, an hour on the ground – that's 14 seats you can sell each way. In the same time, you can do five or six trips to St Mary's, that's 190-230 passengers, so it makes sense to stay local."

The ATC team consists of five controllers, two assistants, a senior controller and deputy senior controller, working a six-day week. It's a highly governed role, with 25 folders full of rules

The Isles of Scilly Skybus began scheduled services from Land's End to St Mary's in 1987, and remains the primary operator of the route

Airport	Route	Operator	Flight time	Flight time
Land's End	St Mary's	Skybus	20 minutes	Year-round
St Mary's	Land's End	Skybus	20 minutes	Year-round
St Mary's	Newquay	Skybus	30 minutes	April – October
St Mary's	Exeter	Skybus	60 minutes	March – October
St Mary's	Penzance	Starspeed	15 minutes	Year-round

Above: Westward Airways aircraft in front of the 1969 terminal building, as opened by actress Elizabeth Taylor
Land's End Airport

Left: The panorama from the Land's End air traffic control tower on a summer day

Land's End Runways	Length	Width	Surface	Notes
02/20	1,591ft (485m)	62ft (19m)	Grass	-
07/25	2,274ft (693m)	59ft (18m)	Tarmac	Grass until July 2014
12/30	1,673ft (510m)	59ft (18m)	Grass	-
16/34	2,572ft (784m)	59ft (18m)	Tarmac	Grass until July 2014

St Mary's Runways	Length	Width	Surface	
14/32	2,287ft (697m)	75ft (23m)	Tarmac	Built in 1991
09/27	1,716ft (523m)	59ft (18m)	Tarmac	Half grass until 2015

tiles add to the mid-Atlantic feel of the interior design.

The airport café overlooks the apron and offers locally sourced food prepared on site – the cakes are scandalously good. Café staff are bubbly and chat to frequent flyers on first name terms. Skybus have two check-in desks with passenger scales (because weight is always an issue), one for Land's End, one for Newquay and Exeter. At the other end of the terminal is the Starspeed check-in for helicopter services to Penzance. There's no

Across the ether

Arriving at St Mary's, baggage is delivered in scarcely more time than it takes to walk to the terminal. Minibuses offer onward connections to other parts of the island, and to boats for transportation to the other islands. The step-free terminal, with a glass fronted facade feels contemporary, perched atop a domed plateau, but at ease in the rural landscape, overlooking the coast in three directions. Inside, white paint and vaulted ceilings create a light, spacious vibe. A wall-mounted post box – an airport rarity these days – and a smattering of comfy leather sofas generate a snug feel. Rows of blue seating and pin-striped carpet

Arriving at St Mary's, baggage is delivered in scarcely more time than it takes to walk to the terminal

St Mary's history

Lying one mile from Hugh Town, the airport is run by the Council of the Isles of Scilly and owned by the Duchy of Cornwall, which makes it unique in being the only UK airport owned by the heir to the throne.

After the first Dragon touched down in 1937, establishing the airlink with the mainland, aviation on St Mary's gradually developed. The airport moved from the golf course to land at High Cross Farm in August 1939, and by the end of 1949 the Ministry of Transport had built an ATC tower and waiting room to form the first terminal.

Flights from Plymouth and Exeter began in 1961, and a service to Gatwick was initiated in 1963, with the first Newquay service departing in 1966. Brymon Airways began operations to Newquay and Plymouth in 1972, adding Exeter to the network the following year, and would be resident until September 29, 1990. In 1987 Skybus began scheduled services from Land's End to St Mary's and have become part of the furniture, currently operating to Land's End, Newquay and Exeter.

In 1959, Harold Wilson built a very modest holiday home close to the airport. In 1975 and by this time, Prime Minister, he was invited to open the new terminal, which he used to commute to the mainland to catch the train from Penzance to London. After leaving Downing Street he spent an increasing amount of time on the island and is buried in the local churchyard. The current terminal opened in 2015.

St Mary's airport café overlooks the apron and offers locally sourced food – the cakes are scandalously good

denying it's a friendly airport and the attitude of the staff is exemplified by Greg Simpson, who is check-in, ground handler, despatcher, and unofficial tourist information guide.

Island life

Tamar Smethurst has worked at St Mary's since 2009, and holds the positions of deputy airport manager and air traffic controller. She told me: "The airport is bigger than when I was a kid, they did a big refit in 2015. We used to have model aircraft hanging from the ceiling, which I miss, we had terracotta tiled floors and 50s style buses."

The route network extends to Land's End, Exeter, Newquay and Penzance heliport but she revealed flight operations vary with the seasons: "In darkest winter we might go down to six Skybus and four helicopter flights a day. In the summer, that will triple and quadruple, particularly over gig weekends – one of our busiest periods of the year, is the World Pilot Gig Championships." (Gigs are six-oared wooden boats)

Because the airfield is on a domed plateau, Smethurst revealed: "We sometimes get a few panicked general aviation (GA) aircraft landing on 09 because they can't see the full runway, just the top of the hill, and think 'I don't know how much is on the other end of that… I'm gonna' slam on the anchors.'" The southeastern end of 14/32 is close to 50-60ft high granite cliffs and there's a footpath crossing nearby too – a bell rings and lights flash to warn walkers of imminent arrivals or departures.

Recalling the effects of COVID-19, Smethurst said: "It hit us like it did all airports but we did stay open because we're a lifeline link and had at least one scheduled flight per day for absolutely necessary travel. We did see a quite resurgence as soon as everything opened up, because there was a big boost in staycations."

The ATC team consists of four people, two of whom are 'homegrown': "We started out as assistants and have been trained up here. We provide aerodrome and approach procedural control – 4,000ft and below, generally." They work a six-day week with no Sunday flying: "In the summer we're 8am-6.30pm, so the early person will start at 7.30am and finish at 4pm, and the late person will start at 10am."

Although there is almost no night flying, Smethurst said: "Scheduled operators can request extensions, and if we've got the air traffic and fire crew staff to do it, we will. For night flights, which are mostly medevacs, we have an out of hours on-call person who will come in and turn on the lights. If the weather is terrible, they've got the option to [ask for] a controller, and one of us will come in." All of which means the ATC team have homes nearby: "Most of us live close to the airfield, so it's work and play. It's lovely in the summer, when we've got visiting GA and a menagerie of aircraft out there. I swear my five-year-old is better at aircraft 'rec' than I am!"

Smethurst explained the practicalities of extending the runways make expansion unlikely: "I'm not sure we

Starspeed Sikorsky S-76C, G-IOSH (c/n 760657) arriving at St Mary's after a 15 minute flight from Penzance heliport

Helicopters

On May 1, 1964, BEA introduced the UK's first scheduled helicopter service, operating a solitary Sikorsky S-61 on the Land's End to St Mary's route. The operation was transferred to the new Penzance heliport on September 1, 1964, and then after the BEA-BOAC merger, it was renamed British Airways Helicopters in March 1974. On July 16, 1983, tragedy occurred on final approach to St Mary's when G-BEON (c/n 61770) crashed into calm seas in poor visibility, 1.5 miles short of land – only six of the 26 people aboard survived.

When privatised in 1986, it was purchased by media tycoon Robert Maxwell and renamed British International Helicopters. The route was discontinued on October 31, 2012, and Penzance heliport was sold off to become a branch of Sainsbury's. Helicopter flights resumed in the summer of 2020, from the new Penzance heliport on Jelbert Way and are currently operated by Starspeed flying a pair Sikorsky S-76Cs, G-PNZE (c/n 760689), and G-IOSH (c/n 760657).

Above: The terminal exterior at St Mary's has a modern look that blends with the rural surroundings

Left: A relaxed, mid-Atlantic vibe defines the terminal at St Mary's

can unless we 'do a Madeira' and build [14/32] out into the sea. There's not much space – 09/27 is the shortest, but it's quite a steep hill. At the 27 end it drops away even further, so that makes it even steeper, and at the 09 end we've got houses so we can't extend that way." Runway length limits the aircraft, which reduces the range: "Twin Otters and PC-12s are pretty much the biggest we can get in here. Legend has it that a Dash 8 landed here once, with all of its seats and stuff stripped out, many, many years ago."

With the physical geographic limitations restricting flights to short hops to the mainland, Smethurst explained access to new routes is likely to be through connecting flights from existing destinations: "We are what we are, but maybe that's partly why people come here, because it's unique. The novelty of flying in such small aircraft; people say 'I flew in this tiny aircraft called the Twin Otter', and the helicopters as well, I think that's a big pull for us. A bit different, bit quirky.

"We all work together as one team at the airport; our main objective is to service the islands and the locals, and we're all really dedicated to it. This is our community and there's great respect for the guys who work here. It's not a big airport, but has its own challenges, and everyone really is a jack of all trades, has to wear so many hats, and do so many different jobs at the same time."

The final whistle

The staff at both airports are close knit communities, where positive attitudes and a willingness to multi-task are key to smooth operations – a cheerful part of the journey, not just a functional component of it. The thrill of flying small aircraft to remote parts of the UK is unlikely to go out of fashion for the enthusiast – and the experience is all the more joyous because of it.

The sight of a warm orange sunset and the sound of squawking seagulls outside Penzance station signalled boarding time for the 9.45pm 'Night Riviera' back to Paddington. Those big diesel engines rumbled into life and the conductor blew his whistle… ✈

Over the Cornish landscape and Sennen Cove on an inbound flight to Land's End

Connecting
canyons *and* capitals

As the closest airport to the Grand Canyon with a commercial air service, Flagstaff/Pulliam has quite the tourist attraction on its doorstep. **Thomas Haynes** travels to the Arizona facility to find out about its unique operation

With the Grand Canyon and a university with 30,000 students on its doorstep, Flagstaff Pulliam Airport (FLG) has all the ingredients of a thriving regional gateway. Situated some 150 miles north and a two- to three-hour drive from Phoenix, the facility is an important asset to the city of Flagstaff, allowing residents easy access to the state capital. For tourists, FLG is the closest airport to the Grand Canyon with a commercial air service and is currently served by American Airlines' regional brand American Eagle.

Situated to the south of the city, the facility caters for both general aviation and airline traffic. With a single runway (21/03) that spans 8,800ft in length and 150ft in width, the site is notable for its elevation, which tops 7,015ft above sea level. On summer days, the density altitude can surpass 10,000ft, which when paired with the high terrain in the vicinity, makes it a complex environment for some aircraft.

The most common visitors to the airport are American Eagle Bombardier CRJ-700s operated by SkyWest Airlines on behalf of American Airlines. The gateway also regularly handles large civil and military types, including Boeing 757s and C-17s.

The terminal building – which opened in 1993 and is positioned at a 45° angle to the runway and single parallel taxiway – offers access to three aircraft parking stands. All the necessary facilities are present inside, including check-in desks (which number three), car rental counters (which outstrip the check-in desks), a single baggage belt, TSA security area with two lanes and a waiting room with two gates.

History

Airline flights to the airport date back to 1948, when the facility was opened. Arizona Airways launched an air service with Douglas DC-3s, but after merging with Frontier Airlines in 1950, the Convair CV-340 and CV-580 began to make appearances. During the 1950s ↘

Flagstaff's single runway 21/03 measures 8,800ft in length
Flagstaff Airport

The facility was opened on July 30, **1948** *All images Key-Thomas Haynes unless stated*

The terminal in use today opened in 1993

and 1960s, air service expanded to include direct flights to Denver, Colorado via Gallup in New Mexico, Farmington, New Mexico, and Durango, Colorado. However, Frontier flights came to an end in 1979.

During this time and through to the early 1980s, several commuter carriers played a crucial role in connecting Flagstaff primarily to Phoenix. These included Cochise Airlines, Desert Air Service, Desert Pacific Airlines, Sun West Airlines and SkyWest Airlines. Aircraft ranging from Fairchild Swearingen Metroliners and Beechcraft C99s to de Havilland Canada DHC-6 Twin Otters, Cessna 402s and Piper Navajos were a common sight at the airport during this period.

American Eagle, operated by Wings West Airlines, represented American Airlines in Flagstaff from 1986 to 1987, using Metroliners for flights to Phoenix. Meanwhile, America West Airlines made its entrance in 1987, operating De Havilland Canada DHC-8 Dash 8s. Flights to the carrier's hubs in Phoenix and Las Vegas, with the latter making a stop at Grand Canyon National Park Airport, followed. On the occasions, Flagstaff would be treated to the use of Boeing 737-200s by America West, which would fill in as a back-up for the Dash 8s. The operation was handed over to Phoenix-based Mesa Airlines in 1992, which flew Beechcraft 1900Ds and Embraer EMB120 Brasilias, flying

as America West Express between FLG and Phoenix.

By 1996, the airport saw up to 16 daily flights to the state capital, with one departing every hour. The services were upgauged to the Dash 8 in 1998. Following America West's merger with US Airways in 2007, the flights were rebranded as US Airways Express.

A significant milestone for Flagstaff came in 2012, when all of its flights were upgraded to the 50-seat Bombardier CRJ-200, signifying the first time in its history that jet aircraft were regularly scheduled to serve the airport. Following the 2015 merger of US Airways with American Airlines, American Eagle service returned to

FLG. The Phoenix flights received a further upgrade in 2017, when the CRJ-200 was swapped out for the larger 70-seat CRJ-700, operated by SkyWest Airlines. During 2018, a single Saturday flight to Los Angeles was added, utilising a CRJ-700 operated by SkyWest as American Eagle. United Airlines joined the line-up in 2019, when it launched a daily flight to Denver using Embraer ERJ145s. The service ended in October 2022.

Current picture

At present, American Eagle is the airport's only airline partner and offers a daily flight to Dallas/Fort Worth, four to five daily services to Phoenix/Sky Harbor and a weekly Saturday connection to Los Angeles, which returned after a hiatus in October 2024.

Despite having the Grand Canyon on its doorstep, and a thriving city of more than 70,000 residents, airport management say there's one thing that is holding them back, although it is out of their control.

Brian Gall, director of Flagstaff Airport, explained: "The major challenge we're facing at the moment is the regional airline pilot shortage. The United [Denver] service here was very successful with an 83% load factor in the final year of operation and as many as three flights a day to Denver. Unfortunately, both American and United, along with our other partners that haven't flown to Flagstaff before, have shifted a lot of their pilots to their mainline operations, where they can fly more passengers with the same number of crew, so we're feeling the effects of that."

The number of American flights is slightly reduced from where it was three or four years ago but, as demonstrated by the reintroduction of the Los Angeles service, FLG is starting to see it tick back up. Gall said more than five million tourists visit the region each year, but because of the airport's proximity to Phoenix, it suffers a 78% 'leakage rate' to Sky Harbor, meaning that 78% of the people who want to arrive in Flagstaff are choosing to fly to Phoenix and then drive up.

Through its 'Fly Flagstaff First' campaign, the airport is encouraging locals to consider travelling through FLG when they're flying out. The facility's director also believes that by adding ↘

In addition to airline traffic, the airport has a sizeable GA population

The Bombardier CRJ-700 is the only airliner regularly scheduled to operate to and from Flagstaff

a second airline, customer choice will increase, lowering ticket prices – which are currently marginally higher than Phoenix, which is typical for regional airports compared to major US hubs. However, the author found that on a connecting international itinerary via Phoenix beginning in London, the leg to Flagstaff made no real difference to the overall price.

In a move to sweeten any possible airline deal, airport management have applied for federal funding to help with revenue and advertising support for a new air carrier at the facility. Gall said he had had conversations with "a number of different air carriers", and that he was hoping to get additional air service "mostly to places north and northeast of Flagstaff."

Around 80,000 passengers travelled through FLG during 2024. As a result of the pilot shortage and a reduction in flights, this figure is down on the all-time record of 124,000 in 2019. "I think that that's a position we could find ourselves in again very soon," admitted Gall. "I don't think it's going to take a lot of things to go our way before we start to see numbers near where we were at our peak."

Throughout its recent history, legacy carriers have dominated the airline offering at FLG, so could there be a place for a low-cost operator? Gall thinks so: "In fact we've had conversations with some of them. However, some of the challenges we face are that a lot of our traffic is tourist traffic and the low-cost carriers tend to fly between one and three times per week, which can make scheduling a little bit challenging. Also, in our case, being as close as we are to Phoenix/Sky Harbor, I could see some of those passengers opting to fly to Phoenix instead of coming here, but I do think that there's an opportunity for a low-cost carrier to come to a place like Flagstaff."

Another challenge for the airport that rolls around like clockwork every year is winter. The facility's positioning at high elevation means that clearing snow is a major part of daily operations during the colder months. Gall said: "We have a lot of sunny days punctuated by really intense snowfall. We might get four to six inches, maybe even up to a foot sometimes, and then some sunny days after that. Moving that volume of snow in a short period of time can be challenging.

Flagstaff's Airport Rescue Fire Fighting (ARFF) and Operations team provides 24-hour year-round coverage

The terminal's check-in area has just three counters

Bombardier CRJ-701ER, N715SK (c/n 10179), takes off from runway 21 at Flagstaff

We frequently get snowfall rates that exceed two inches an hour. With the amount of pavement we have out here, keeping the equipment staffed, keeping people on top of it to stop the snow from getting too deep is the main point of emphasis for us."

With the pilot shortage impacting current operations, where does the airport director think the facility will be in a decade's time? "In ten years, I could easily see us in a position where we have an additional carrier or two, and our enplanements moving up to somewhere in the mid-100 region. That's going to trigger the need for some things like terminal expansion projects and those take some time to get off the ground. So I'm not sure if that will be done in ten years, but I could see us being pretty far on the planning stage on some of that, along with the increased amount of traffic that would entail."

With its cosy and intimate feel, FLG has everything a passenger would want. Now it just needs more flight options, which is something management are working very hard to achieve.

Above: FedEx Feeder operates cargo flights between Phoenix/Sky Harbor and Flagstaff

Left: There's no searching around for the correct baggage carousel at Flagstaff as it only has one!

The author's ride for the return flight to Phoenix, American Eagle CRJ-701ER, N702SK (c/n 10136), is prepared for departure

Flagstaff experience

The author travelled through Flagstaff to reach the Grand Canyon in early September 2024. After touching down, passengers deplane onto the tarmac and then walk the short distance to the arrivals door, which then leads straight into the baggage reclaim area. There was no searching around for the correct carousel and very minimal waiting time for the bags. The car rental counters are perfectly positioned on the other side of the room, then it's a short stroll to the car park, which is positioned about 100ft from the terminal exit door. The whole experience – which was extremely smooth – lasted no more than 20 minutes.

For the author's departure from Flagstaff, a visit was paid to the check-in desks located at the western end of the terminal. The agent manning the desk – who would later don a hi-vis vest and assume ground crew duties – explained the slightly different bag check process, which involves passengers placing their suitcases on a metal roller track and pushing them through a hole in the wall themselves. There was no queue for the TSA and, in a matter of minutes, we were in the departure lounge awaiting the aircraft's arrival. Once the aircraft had parked, the large windows offered a front row seat to watch all aspects of the turnaround at close range. It was even possible to spot our bags being loaded on the aircraft. It wasn't long before boarding commenced and we were on our way to Phoenix/Sky Harbor.

Having also driven between Phoenix and Flagstaff during my trip, I can safely say that flying was significantly more enjoyable.

The ghost of
Aeropuerto

Located some 140 miles south of the Spanish capital, the €1.1bn Ciudad Real International Airport was intended to alleviate some of the pressures at Madrid/Barajas. However, the plan failed. **Lee Cross** examines one of Europe's most infamous "ghost airports"

Don Quijote

Planned during economic glory years, Ciudad Real International Airport opened when Spain was going through one of its worst economic recessions in history and subsequently became one of the country's most infamous "ghost airports" *Getty Images/Javier Soriano*

A map highlighting the location of Ciudad Real International Airport and its distance from the Spanish capital *Key-Robert Veitch*

The massive runway at Ciudad Real is 13,450ft (4,100m) long and 200ft (60m) wide and was built to handle the Airbus A380 *CRIA*

The idea for an airport in the Spanish municipality of Ciudad Real, in the autonomous community of Castilla-La Mancha, first came about in the late 1990s. At the time, Spain had caught the developing wave of an economic boom. Money was plentiful and, as the new millennium arrived, countless construction plans for housing and infrastructure projects – an area that had seen decades of underinvestment – were given the green light.

Tourism was also booming, boosted by the arrival of low-cost airlines, bringing more visitors than ever to its shores. Plans for more than 20 new airports across the country were put forward, including one in Ciudad Real. Swept up in this wave, planners believed the boom times would never end, and that low-cost carriers would serve these new facilities and bring people and thus prosperity to the regions.

The plan for Ciudad Real, Spain's first privately owned airport, was simple: design and build a new facility with a massive runway capable of handling the mighty Airbus A380, which at the time was believed to be the future of commercial air travel. Studies commissioned revealed the hub would create up to 6,000 jobs and massively boost the local economy.

The airport would be linked to the new Madrid-Seville high-speed railway line, becoming the first in the country to be directly connected to the TVE network

and bringing it within reach of the Spanish capital in around 50 minutes with up to 27 trains per hour.

Backed by the Ciudad Real Chamber of Commerce and with several private investors on board – including local savings banks Caja Sur and Caja Castilla-La-Mancha, whose boards were made up of local politicians – work began in earnest on Ciudad Real International Airport, also known as Aeropuerto Don Quijote, named after the local hero of Miguel Cervantes' famous novel. Indeed, plans were also being discussed to build an entertainment park dubbed the 'Kingdom of Don Quijote', which would house Spain's biggest casino.

Air Berlin was one of the airport's earliest operators, offering flights to Palma de Mallorca *CRIA*

An airport to rival Barajas

A 65,000m² passenger apron was built next to the state-of-the-art 28,000m² glass-walled terminal, designed by UK engineering firm RPS Newark and Spanish consultants Aertec Solutions. It would be capable of handling approximately ten million passengers each year and was built around low-cost carrier requirements. With more than three million cubic metres of earth to be moved for the entire construction project, RPS had to ensure the design had minimal impact on the local environment, which included detailed and extensive drainage modelling.

In addition to passenger facilities, the airport would boast expansive general aviation and cargo aprons capable of handling up to 90,000 tonnes of freight annually. ↘

Left: The airport was to be connected to the Madrid-Seville high-speed railway line. Sadly, an incomplete walkway from the terminal in the direction of the line was as far as this part of the project got *Getty Images/ Oli Scarff*

Below: Ryanair introduced the first international route, with a thrice-weekly connection to London/Stansted, in June 2010 *Key Collection*

Ciudad Real boasts an expansive cargo apron, which was capable of handling up to 90,000 tonnes of freight annually
CRIA

The then-operator, CR Aeropuertos, believed that a new airport at Ciudad Real could alleviate some of the pressures at Barajas, with predictions of serving 750,000 passengers in the first year, rising to 2.5 million by year three. Early marketing saw the facility dubbed 'Madrid South'. With its business model of flying to secondary airports, Ryanair was immediately targeted as a potential operator. CR Aeropuertos reported that it was in discussions with around a dozen other carriers, offering attractive tariffs and flexible timetables with no night-time curfews or slot restrictions.

The initial plans were for the airport to open its doors in 2004. However, several delays with the project meant that a new launch date was put forward as October 2008. Subsequently, this was delayed again after the Spanish Transport Ministry refused to issue an operating permit due to environmental concerns regarding the runway being located in a protected bird area.

During this time, Madrid/Barajas' new state-of-the-art Terminal 4, one of the world's largest terminal buildings with more than 760,000m^2 of airside and landside structures, had opened its doors, seeing the Spanish flag carrier Iberia and its partners move their operations to the new site. At the same time, two new runways were also inaugurated, easing the pressure on both the existing terminals and the airport's operation as a whole. Ryanair and easyJet, which had previously shown interest in establishing bases at Ciudad Real, subsequently set up shop at Barajas.

Right: Planners believed the airport would serve 750,000 passengers in the first year. Instead, it received just 53,557
Alamy/Associated Press

Right below: The last commercial flight operated by Vueling departed for Barcelona on October 29, 2011
Getty Images/Julian74

The bubble bursts

Spain's economic bubble dramatically burst in 2008, with the country entering one of its worst recessions in living memory. Mass unemployment ensued, the property market collapsed and the banking sector was in crisis, with one of the banks that had backed the airport having to be rescued by the Bank of Spain.

Despite big plans ahead of its grand opening, the airport had secured just one operator, Spanish regional carrier Air Nostrum. Operations finally began on December 22, 2008, with Air Nostrum offering connections to Barcelona and Las Palmas in the Canary Islands. In the first month, 1,116 passengers were handled on these two routes. Air Berlin followed soon after with flights to Palma de Mallorca. But just a year later, both carriers had left.

In June 2010, Ryanair introduced the airport's first international route, a thrice-weekly rotation to London/Stansted. Despite carrying some 22,000 passengers in the first six months, the route was cut in November that year after the airline failed to reach a satisfactory agreement with the airport's operator.

This left Spanish low-cost carrier Vueling as the airport's only operator. The airline launched flights to the airport in November 2010, with four rotations per week to Barcelona and two to Paris/Orly. Palma was later added. However, the latter two were quickly dropped, leaving just a twice-weekly service to Barcelona, that was heavily subsidised by the local government of the region.

Despite the promise that the airport would eventually serve millions of passengers, in 2009, it saw just 53,557 pass through its doors. A year later, the number had dipped to 33,520.

The planned high-speed rail link never came to fruition. An incomplete 980ft (300m) walkway from the terminal in the direction of the planned station was as far as this part of the project got. Instead, it was replaced with a bus service that initially operated every 30 minutes to Ciudad Real and Puertollano. But as the airlines left, the service was also cut to coincide with Vueling's twice-weekly service.

In 2010, the airport was declared bankrupt with debts of €529m. The last commercial flight, operated by Vueling, departed for Barcelona

✈ Ciudad Real International Airport

IATA Code:	CQM
ICAO Code:	LERL
LID Code:	CQM
Location:	Province of Ciudad Real, Spain
Opened:	22/12/2008
Runway:	10/28 13,450ft (4,100m)
Coordinates:	N38°51.38' / W3°58.20'
Previous Operators:	Air Nostrum
	Ryanair
	Air Berlin
	Vueling

on October 29, 2011. For a few months, the airport remained open, handling a number of private flights before finally closing its doors on April 21, 2012.

No planes, trains, but automobiles

For many years, the facility was left to rot in the intense Iberian sun. Huge yellow crosses were painted at each runway to signal its mothballed status. The only visitors were local wildlife and the odd reporter looking to tell the story of Spain's biggest white elephant.

As aircraft moved out, automobiles moved in, and the enormous 13,450ft (4,100m) runway proved to be the perfect location for Lexus to test its LFA sports car. In 2013, the BBC also used the site as a location for its *Top Gear* programme, racing and speed testing several supercars. The same year, Volvo teamed up with movie legend Jean-Claude Van Damme to record an advert for the dynamic steering in its trucks. Acclaimed Spanish writer and film director Pedro Almodóvar also used the airport as the setting for his film *Los Amantes Passajeros* (The Passenger Lovers).

The airport was then put up for sale for €89m, a fraction of the €1.1bn it had cost to build. In 2013, Zaragoza-based start-up Kriber Air Lines announced plans to develop the facility into a cargo and passenger hub, placing a bid for €40m. The deal was rejected as being too low, while Kriber disappeared as quickly as it had started.

Two years later, a group of Chinese-led investors, Tzaneen International, emerged as the only bidders for the facility after it was put up for auction, placing an offer of just €10,000, well below the €56m minimum price set by the receiver. The deal included the runway, land and control tower, but excluded the terminal and car parks, which the group said it would purchase at a later date. Tzaneen said it planned to invest around €100m to transform Don Quijote into a European cargo hub. However, the sale was later rejected by the Spanish courts.

It would be another three years before the airport was finally sold to Ciudad Real International Airport SL for €56.2 million. The new owners reopened the site in September 2019, and it quickly became home to Irish company Direct Aero Services, which opened a maintenance base at the airport, and Spanish firm Jet Aircraft Services, which launched an aircraft dismantling service.

A new lease of life

Then the COVID-19 pandemic hit. Airlines were forced to ground their aircraft and needed somewhere to park them. Ciudad Real was the perfect location, and during this time, airframes were sent to the airport from Iberia, Vueling, South African Airways, Aer Lingus, Cathay Pacific and Virgin Atlantic, including its Star Wars-themed Boeing 747-443, G-VLIP (c/n 32338). The airport also welcomed a number of cargo flights from Guangzhou, China, bringing medical equipment and PPE.

In May 2023, Sabena Technics inaugurated a new maintenance facility, offering aircraft maintenance, storage and recycling options. The plan was to handle the company's activities in Spain and create around 150 direct skilled jobs to handle around 100 aircraft annually. In November, the team welcomed its first aircraft for maintenance, an Airbus A350-900. Despite initial plans to remain on the site until 2048, in March 2024, the MRO provider announced it would abandon the facility after failing to reach a long-term agreement with the new owners.

Today, the skies above Ciudad Real remain quiet, the perfect environment for pilot training. Despite the loss of Sabena Technics, Ciudad Real has shown its potential as a maintenance and aircraft storage facility. Indeed, the facility's current owner, CRIA, said it has embarked on a new phase for the airport "aimed at operational efficiency and economic sustainability". This includes the transition to a mixed-use model, which combines restricted and public operations, allowing a more flexible and efficient management of air traffic.

While commercial flights remain a distant memory, other airports built during the economic boom, such as Castellón–Costa Azahar Airport, now have regular passenger services. CRIA said discussions with several low-cost carriers have recently intensified, and with discussions around a direct rail connection with the Madrid-Seville high-speed rail line, Ciudad Real International could once again offer "an efficient and competitive alternative to Madrid/Barajas". ✈

The airport's current operator said it had embarked on a new phase "aimed at operational efficiency and economic sustainability" *Getty Images/Oli Scarff*

During COVID, numerous airlines sent their aircraft to Ciudad Real for storage, including Virgin Atlantic with several of its Boeing 747-400 fleet *AirTeamImages.com/ Carlos Enamorado*

Postcard from
BERMU[DA]

Aviators looking for a subtropical break offering history, culture, beaches and aircraft, might be keen to follow **Chris Sloan** on a flying visit to the mid–Atlantic paradise of Bermuda

On a map, the Bermuda archipelago appears like tiny specks in the vast North Atlantic Ocean, at the pinnacle of the infamous Bermuda Triangle. The isolated island chain is 568 miles east of North Carolina in the United States and 2,996 miles southwest of London. Its airport, LF Wade International, is the sole commercial facility on the British Overseas Territory; located in St George's Parish, six miles northeast of the capital, Hamilton. Formerly named Bermuda International Airport, the gateway was renamed in 2007 in honour of the late Leonard Frederick Wade, leader of Bermuda's Progressive Labour Party and Member of Parliament.

Until the early 1940s, Bermuda's only aerodrome was a water-based civilian aircraft flying boat facility at Darrell's Island where Pan Am's famed Boeing 314 Flying Clippers made stops in the pre-war era. The land-based airport of today on St David's Island first put down roots back in 1941-42, as a US military airfield, constructed at a cost of $42m. Kindley Air Force Base was used by the US Air Force and the RAF, and a US Naval Air Station was also established in the grounds of the facility.

Early days

In 1946, Kindley Airport opened for civil operations on the part of the airfield previously used by the RAF. A civil air terminal opened in 1948, parts of which ↘

The Skyport Terminal opened on December 9, 2020
Bermuda Airport

were still in use up until 2020. Early airlines included Colonial, Eagle and Pan Am, offering connectivity to New York, BOAC linking to London, and Trans-Canada Airlines (today's Air Canada) operating to Toronto. As Bermuda emerged as a tourist destination in the 1960s more US carriers, including Northeast, TWA and Eastern, began operating services. In 1970, the US Navy assumed control of Kindley, renaming it US Naval Air Station Bermuda. In 1974, it became one of the first airports to implement US preclearance, allowing travellers to complete customs, immigration and agriculture inspections before boarding direct flights to the United States and arriving as domestic passengers. The booming 1980s witnessed the arrival of American, Delta and United, providing additional capacity to the United States.

Having spent an estimated $2bn of US government funds on the airport since its opening, the US Navy transferred full control to the Bermuda government in 1995. It continues to offer support by providing air traffic control services for Atlantic air traffic passing through Bermudan air space, and air traffic approach control services, from its New York Center. The Federal Aviation Administration (FAA) also contributes funding for navigational aids and associated maintenance.

Final approach

The pink LED mood lighting aboard the night time inbound BermudAir flight 2T452 mirrors that of the bus network signs on routes heading into Hamilton. In complete darkness during the 2hrs 35min overwater service from Fort Lauderdale, it's the only visible light, until the first lights of the archipelago are apparent, shortly before touchdown on Bermuda's only operational runway, the 9,713ft long 12/30. It's almost like landing on a very long aircraft carrier, until we turn off the runway and onto one of the 11 taxiways, each 75ft wide, and conforming to ICAO Codes 3 and 4.

Having not visited since 2019, the difference between the old and new terminal is like night and day. There are six airbridge-equipped gates, partitioned between US and international arrivals, and although I was fond of the old tarmac-touching airstairs, since it is raining nostalgia vanishes as the Embraer E175 empties through the glass airbridge. Passengers funnel into the almost empty, light and bright, airy immigration hall, where the walls are styled to represent coral reefs, adding an anticipatory sense of place. With no lengthy queues to clear immigration, but plenty of hospitality, the welcome is warm and appreciated. After bag collection from one of two

available carousels, and customs clearance, the urge to be tempted into some spontaneous rum shopping at Somers Isle Trading Company is resisted... just. It's a 20-minute drive to the accommodation in downtown Hamilton – the only city in Bermuda.

Welcome to paradise

At just 21 square miles in area and 24 miles from end to end, spanning eight main islands, Bermuda is one of the world's smallest territories. The year-round population is approximately 64,600 people, with one of the world's highest per capita incomes. It is renowned for the staggering subtropical beauty of its pink sand beaches, grottos, cliffs, clear waters and world-famous golf courses. History buffs might appreciate the UNESCO world heritage site of St George's Island – one of the oldest English settlements in the western hemisphere, and The Royal Naval Dockyard on Ireland Island. Bermuda remains a high-end destination complete with world-class resorts, vibrant shopping, local art and a thriving culinary scene.

The appeal of year-round temperate weather, sun and surf less than two hours from the US is a key driver in the tourism market. For the Brits the appeal is similar, plus there are familiar cultural elements from the mother country, albeit set in an alien climate. The archipelago's polite, dignified hospitality, cleanliness and safety score high marks.

The tourism boom that began in the 1960s, gradually ebbed away post-millennium, but after years of declining tourism, the airport staged a comeback, welcoming 435,280 passengers in 2019. The COVID-19 pandemic halted the resurgence, but numbers had recovered to 364,676 by the end of 2024. Fortunately, ever-resilient Bermuda still means business, and 85% of its GDP is driven by offshore international business, particularly the reinsurance industry.

The Commissioner's House at The Royal Naval Dockyard on Ireland Island
Bermudair

BermudAir became the archipelago's first airline when it launched in September 2023 with a pair of Embraer E175s, including VQ-BLU (c/n 170000344)
Bermudair

How we've got to now

During 2006, JetBlue launched its service, eventually peaking as the market's number two player, behind American Airlines, but by then the terminal was showing its age. Hurricane damage and unsustainable maintenance costs took their toll, so the Bermudan government made plans in 2008 to replace the tired, overcrowded facility – its clean-sheet terminal masterplan projected to cost almost $500m. Unfortunately, the masterplan coincided with the global economic crisis of 2008-2009 and, with a funding shortfall, the search for a foreign financial partner began. Public-private partnerships (PPP) – joint ventures between governments and private stakeholders – have long been in vogue, and in 2017 the Bermudan government signed a 30-year agreement with Aecon Concessions. The deal with the Canadian firm created the Bermuda ↘

Construction on the new 288,000sq ft Skyport Terminal began in March 2017
Bermuda Airport

> " Bermuda remains a high–end destination complete with world–class resorts, vibrant shopping, local art and a thriving culinary scene "

modifications, plus installation and operation of a new aircraft hydrant refuelling system, with an overall construction cost of $400m. On December 9, 2020, the new Skyport Terminal opened with a ribbon-cutting ceremony and Delta Air Lines flight DL617, inbound from New York/JFK, took the honours as the first aircraft to use the new terminal.

As of June 2025, aviation analytics data from Cirium indicates seven airlines operate nonstop services to 21 destinations: 17 in the US, three in Canada, and London/Heathrow. In terms of available seats, New York/JFK is the number one destination. The Boeing 777s flown by British Airways on the Heathrow runs are the sole widebodies using the facility. Airbus A320 and Boeing 737 family aircraft constitute the bulk of scheduled traffic, though there's a lively executive jet scene due to the presence of high net-worth individuals and offshore corporations on the islands. BermudAir became the archipelago's first airline when it launched in September 2023, operating a pair of E175s (see *Airliner World* May 2025). It offers the second-highest number of seats at the airport, plus year-round connectivity to ten destinations in the US and three in Canada – Toronto/Pearson and Boston/Logan are the only routes where it faces direct competition.

The airport is susceptible to operational challenges due to isolation and sometimes unpredictable weather. For example, the closest diversion is located

Skyport Corporation, and covered the redevelopment of the air passenger terminal building and its ongoing maintenance and operations. At the end of the contract, complete control, ownership and revenue of Skyport revert to the Bermudan government. The Bermuda Airport Authority supervises airport operations, quality standards and other performance obligations of the airport operator, and provides air traffic control operations, meteorological services, airport fire and rescue services and ground electronics.

Though the scale and cost of the project were scaled back considerably, construction on the new 288,000sq ft terminal, priced at $274m, began in March 2017. The package also included the construction and operation of additional apron space, installation of the apron lighting system and taxiway

US side for our return home to Miami via Orlando, we discover a small but bespoke and very local selection of shops, bars and restaurants. Each gate operates in a common-use configuration with emphasis on the customer experience, offering sweeping views of the tarmac, abundant comfortable seating and AC power. There are four gates in the US departures area and two in international, but the configuration can be adapted in the event of all US or all international flights. The terminal was built with six contact stands, with six remote stands on the old terminal apron, though these are used rarely.

It's a relatively compact building, but feels much larger due to the high ceilings, sweeping glass facades, natural light, spacious layout and, on this occasion, a distinct lack of people. We don't take advantage of many of the amenities, except for the sparkling clean restrooms, because my ticket comes with complimentary admission to the locally owned and operated Primeclass Lounge. This intimate lounge is beautifully appointed with lovely hospitality, to the point that I begin to hope for a flight delay to enjoy the lounge more.

With departure time approaching, it's a short walk from the lounge to the gate, onto the glass airbridge and into my waiting E175. The cabin LED lights were now lit a cool shade of blue, to match the bus stops on the route from Hamilton to the airport. After a short take-off run, our jet tipped its wing to say farewell, and we enjoyed one final glance at the craggy and coral beauty that is Bermuda. ✈

Each gate operates in a common-use configuration with emphasis on the customer experience, offering sweeping views of the tarmac and abundant comfortable seating
Chris Sloan

Left: The old departure lounge is a far cry from its 21st century replacement
Chris Sloan

Below: American Airlines operates services to Charlotte, Miami, New York/JFK, Philadelphia and Washington/National
Bermuda Airport

nearly 600 miles away so inbound aircraft have to load enough fuel to get to Bermuda plus enough to make it to the East Coast of the US and the allocated diversion airfield.

Bon voyage

After a few days of sightseeing, it was time for the author to head home to Florida – along The Causeway, crossing over Castle Harbour and onto Long Bird Island at Bermuda's eastern end. The approaching, contemporary architecture of the Skyport Terminal is accentuated with Bermudan twists, including sloping roof angles and triangles, making quite an impression in contrast to the abandoned, dilapidated, original terminal, which still stands next door.

On a quiet Sunday afternoon during the low season, the light and welcoming check-in hall, with 29 check-in counters, is at its most calming as we approach the BermudAir desks. The airport offers an exclusive concierge fast-track service for seamless, escorted arrivals and departures. Though tempted by The Whistling Frog Rum Bar and Grill, instead we quickly glide through US preclearance and security checks, which

are even smoother than those of the Transportation Security Administration (TSA). It is one of two security checkpoints, with the other allocated to international departures.

Once airside, the terminal is split between US customs preclearance, and international for passengers to Canada and the United Kingdom. Ushered to the

There has been an airfield at Nice in one form or another since 1902, when the rocky beach was used to test gliders. In the 1920s it was known as California Airfield, then after World War Two the DNA of the modern facility began to evolve. During the 1970s, a land reclamation project enabled the development of the facility that greets visitors today, processing 14,770,626 passengers during 2024, with an extension to Terminal 2 opening in 2025 *Aeroports de la Cote dAzur/J.Kelagopian*

637/25

THE DESTINATION FOR
AVIATION ENTHUSIASTS

Visit us today and discover all our publications

Aviation News is renowned for providing the best coverage of every branch of aviation.

and subscribe to your favourite magazine...
/collections/subscriptions

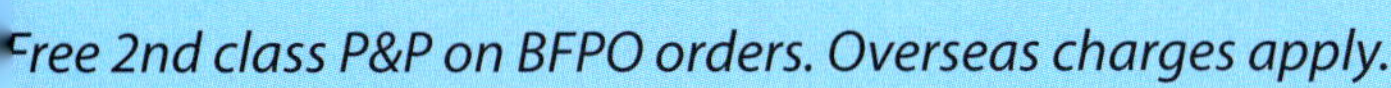

Free 2nd class P&P on BFPO orders. Overseas charges apply.

Eurohub

The Eurohub complex was built to the south of the main terminal building and officially opened to the public on July 22, 1991 *Birmingham Airport Archive*

n July 1991, Birmingham Airport's (BHX) innovative 'Eurohub' complex opened for passenger services. While the facility may no longer be a standalone terminal, its ground-breaking design and operation became a benchmark for future airport planning.

To better understand why Eurohub came to be, it's important to put the development in the context of the wider changes taking place at BHX in the 1980s. Birmingham Airport opened its new £29m 'Main Terminal' in April 1984. Capable of handling three million passengers per year, the West Midlands site presented itself as a viable alternative to London/Heathrow for airlines and passengers alike.

Situated northeast of the main runway, across from the former Elmdon terminal, the location was chosen not only because of its proximity to the recently opened National Exhibition Centre (NEC) and railway station (linking both Birmingham and London via the West Coast Main Line) but also because of its ample room for expansion.

At the time, Birmingham was the UK's fifth busiest gateway and one of the fastest-growing in the country. Passenger traffic in the immediate years after the terminal's opening grew much quicker than expected, rising by 114% from 1.63 million per year in 1985 to 3.49 million in 1990.

It wasn't just traveller numbers growing either. Airline operators also increased, from eight in 1983 to 20 by 1989. Scheduled destinations served also blossomed – from 24 in 1983 to 39 by the end of the decade. Arguably a victim of its own success, a building that had originally been set to cope with demand well into the 1990s was becoming overcrowded and a solution was desperately needed.

Regional connections

Aviation in the UK was very different in the 1980s to what it is today. Point-to-point flights from the British regions to Europe were almost non-existent, as were the big-name, low-cost

and **spoke**

The former Eurohub terminal at Birmingham airport revolutionised hub and spoke operations in the UK and Europe. **Lee Cross** examines the history behind the facility

airlines that would eventually go on to operate them.

British Airways (BA) had been struggling with its regional business for many years. Following privatisation in 1987, management were keen to streamline its network and looked across the pond to the United States and its 'hub-and-spoke' concept.

Rather than introducing direct flights from airports such as Edinburgh, Glasgow and Belfast, BA saw the possibility of seamlessly routing domestic passengers through its Birmingham and, later, Manchester (MAN) bases and onwards to Europe.

Initial trials had proved successful and the airline was keen to develop the initiative further. At the time, BHX was a key hub for British Airways and had ample capacity compared to slot-congested Heathrow. In real terms, establishing a hub-and-spoke system in Birmingham for its European connections allowed BA to free up slots in London that could be used for more lucrative long-haul flights.

For BHX, the addition of transfer passengers would mean that destinations that previously may not have been viable from local traffic alone could now be added. This was on top of the potential for additional frequencies on existing routes. It seemed like a win-win for both the airline and the site.

Enter the Eurohub

Encouraged by recent growth, in February 1988, an announcement was made that a new hub facility would be built at Birmingham to be used exclusively by British Airways and its partner airlines. While the top-line concept sounded simple enough, designers had to factor in the complexity of customs and immigration requirements for passengers transferring between the UK and another European country. Convention at the time suggested that this would demand separate buildings. But standalone terminals would have a huge impact on the already severe time constraints for transferring travellers, ↘

British Airways transferred 26 Boeing 737-236s to its regional divisions at Birmingham and Manchester, with some having titles added to their fuselage to denote their base *AirTeamImages.com/ Carl Ford*

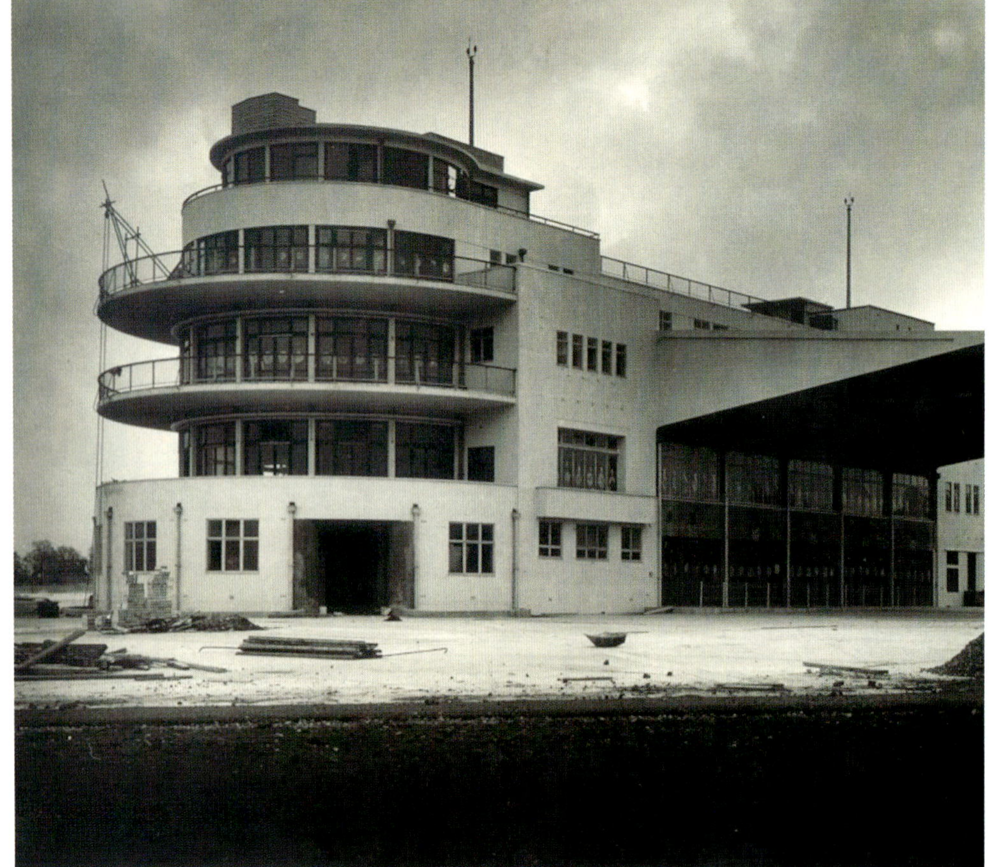

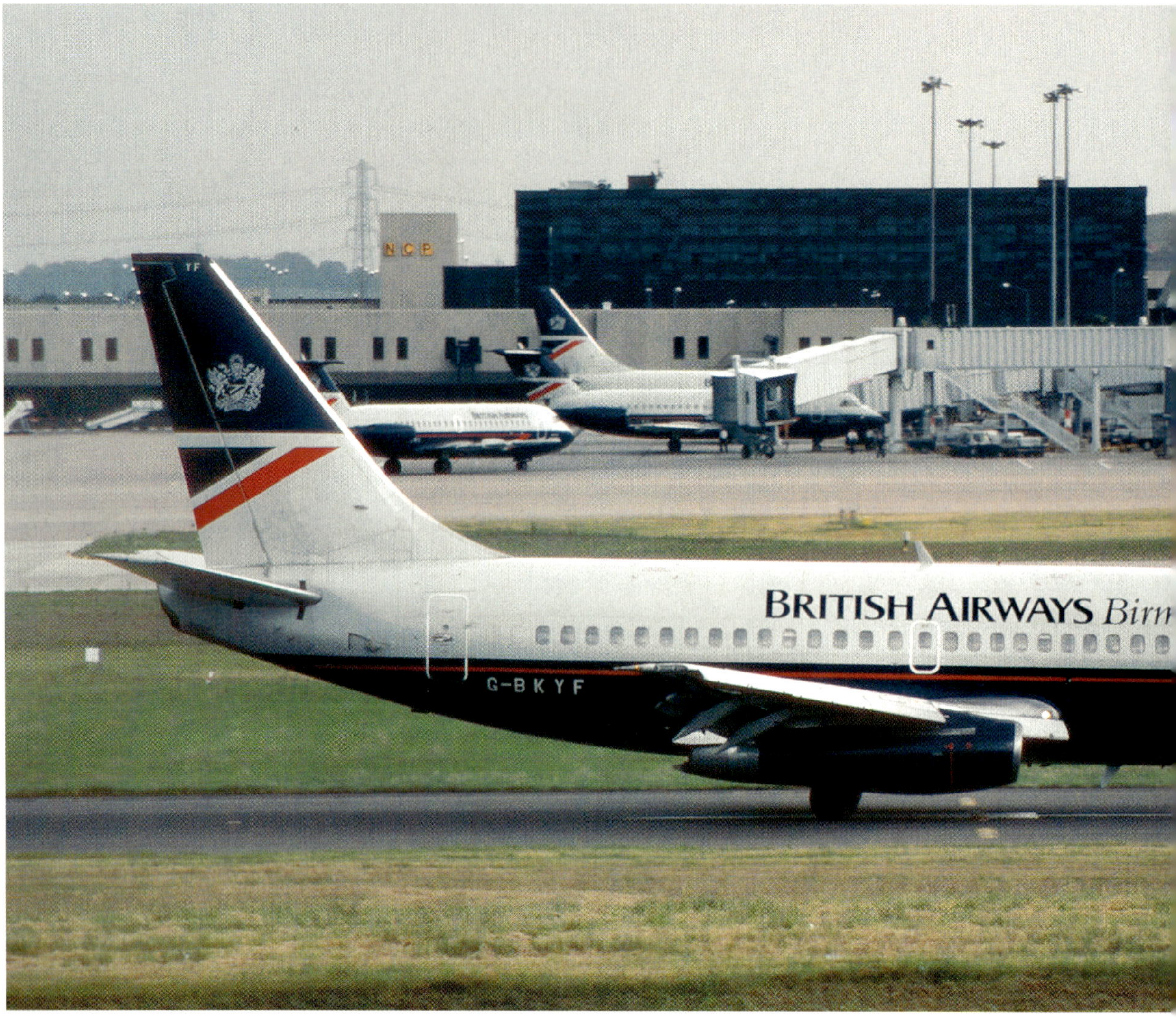

The original Elmdon complex was officially opened in July 1939 *Birmingham Airport Archive*

going completely against BA's plan for speedy, seamless connections.

Three potential sites were earmarked, including a satellite at the end of the domestic pier, expansion of the existing terminal by building out onto the apron, or a brand-new structure located to the south that would completely replace the domestic facility. The latter site was eventually selected and the initial 'back of the envelope' sketches became reality when construction began in September 1989.

It wasn't just the building itself that broke the mould. A further innovation was the way in which the development was funded. A joint venture company was established that comprised Birmingham Airport, which owned 25% of the shares; BA and National Car Parks (NCP) at 21.4% each; developer John Laing Partners on 11.9%; the Forte Group, who controlled the retail and catering facilities in the terminal with 6%; and finally the seven West Midlands District Councils were given the remaining 14.3%.

Less than two years after construction began, the £60m state-of-the-art Eurohub opened its doors on July 22, 1991, ahead of schedule and under budget. To mark the occasion, a special ceremony was held with British

Queen Elizabeth II opened Birmingham Airport's new £29m 'Main Terminal' in April 1984
Birmingham Airport Archive

The Eurohub concept tried to bring hub-and-spoke traffic to the West Midlands
Birmingham Airport Archive

Many features we take for granted in modern airports today were first realised at the site
Birmingham Airport Archive

Airways's flagship Concorde, G-BOAD (c/n 210), in attendance, along with the Duchess of York, deputy chairman and CEO of British Airways, Sir Colin Marshall, and Birmingham Airport's CEO, Sir Robert (Bob) Taylor.

Speaking at the event, Taylor said: "I'm delighted to say British Airways and its partners, Birmingham European Airways and Brymon, have introduced this very exciting hub-and-spoke venture. A new venture for the UK, and indeed Europe."

Eurohub wasn't simply a milestone in the history of BHX or British Airways, it had truly global significance. The ambition of its developers meant the hub-and-spoke venture was taken a step further, and it became the first terminal in the world to integrate domestic and international arrivals. The three-storey building had a split-level operation with a series of external ramps that handled both arriving and departing passengers, as well as securing connecting traffic. For added flexibility, each gate was capable of serving domestic or international arrivals or departures.

Compactness was key, with maximum transfer times of just 30 minutes built into the airlines' schedules. This was aided by the use of the latest

'BA Regional' to improve the profitability of services from Birmingham, Manchester, Scotland and Northern Ireland. Twenty-six Boeing 737-236s would be transferred to BHX and MAN to replace its ageing BAC One-Eleven fleet. Some even had 'Birmingham' or 'Manchester' titles added to their fuselage to denote their base.

Birmingham European went on to become Maersk Air UK in August 1993, following a failed merger with Brymon, with Maersk taking the BA/BEA partnership a step further by becoming a full British Airways franchise. In 2003, Maersk UK was put up for sale, and through a management buyout, the airline became Duo Airways in June that year. Operations continued from Eurohub, but in November, its long-standing agreement with British Airways was terminated. Sadly Duo was a short-lived venture and ceased operations on May 1, 2004.

Above: **Brymon European Airways supported BA's mainline operation at the hub** *AirTeamImages.com/ Keith Blincow*

Right: **Eurohub was also utilised by BA's other partner airlines, such as Caledonian Airways** *Birmingham Airport Archive*

While the site is best remembered for connecting traffic, it also handled a significant number of point-to-point passengers *Birmingham Airport Archive*

technology, including automatic ticketing and boarding passes.

There was also a centrally controlled door operation system, creating what was known as a 'valving operation.' A series of secure doors could be opened and closed as required, moving flows of passengers between aircraft and terminal facilities, something now commonplace in airports globally but completely pioneering at the time.

Serving 'Boomingham'

Eurohub was capable of handling 2.5 million passengers per year, and provisions were made for a second phase, increasing capacity to four million, should demand require it. The proportion of transfer traffic was also expected to increase from the previous 26%, to 35% within the first four years. In reality, traffic grew much faster than expected, and more than 800,000 customers passed through the terminal to 18 destinations in year one.

As expected, British Airways was able to synergise its network at BHX. The airline stopped its Amsterdam route and entered a codeshare agreement with Birmingham European Airways (BEA), which immediately increased its schedule. BA also reduced its flights to Belfast, with BEA stepping in to fill the gap by launching a new link to the Northern Irish capital, also under a codeshare agreement.

So successful was the new facility that British Airways ran an advertising campaign using the tagline 'Boomingham', highlighting the extensive number of flights from the UK's second city. At its peak BA, along with its then partner airlines BEA, Brymon Airways and Caledonian Airways, was carrying some 40% of the airport's scheduled traffic.

In March 1992, British Airways announced the formation of

Officially opened in 1991, the site allowed smooth flight transfers *Birmingham Airport Archive*

In 1999, British Airways introduced the first of its brand-new Airbus A319 fleet at Birmingham. The arrival of the ninth example in June 1999 meant that the last of its 737-200s could then be retired from the base.

A further reorganisation of BA's regional operations and the creation of British Airways Citiexpress in March 2002 saw the A319s leave Birmingham for Heathrow, where they were used to replace the airline's 737-400 examples. This fleet was then transferred to London/Gatwick, replacing the ex-CityFlyer Avro RJ100s, which were in turn moved to BHX. The introduction of the smaller RJ100s meant an immediate 9% reduction in capacity by BA at Eurohub.

Terminal upgrades

On March 3, 2000, the new £40m 'Millennium Link' was opened by Her Majesty The Queen and the Duke of Edinburgh. The redevelopment saw a brand new frontage covering both terminals and their interconnection via a two-storey arrivals concourse for the first time.

The following year, Eurohub celebrated its tenth birthday. Since opening in 1991, the terminal had welcomed 17.85 million passengers and had handled approximately 355,500 aircraft movements. By 2001, 24 destinations were available, and some 1.8 million passengers per year were being handled, an increase of 125% from 1991. Rod Eddington, BA's then chief executive, visited for a special ceremony to mark the occasion, which included a birthday cake in the form of a British Airways A319.

Speaking at the time, Eddington said: "There are more services to more European destinations by British Airways than by any other carrier at Birmingham. In enhancing and developing services for Midland travellers, we and our partners have invested more than £1bn, and we remain committed to the development of a profitable network at Birmingham."

Further investment was made by introducing electronic ticketing and self-service check-in machines and opening a new and expanded terraces lounge for premium travellers.

Despite Eddington's positive spin regarding operations from Birmingham, the airline's regional arm continued to be unprofitable. British Airways had sold its shares in the terminal following restructuring in March 1997, which led to the airport becoming a private company.

In February 2006, British Airways Citiexpress became BA Connect, the flag carrier's attempt to compete with the growing number of low-cost airlines. Alas, just nine months later, it was announced that BA Connect would be taken over by Flybe.

On March 25, 2007, the BA Connect name disappeared, along with the BA flight code, from Birmingham's departure board after 68 illustrious years. The Eurohub moniker was also quietly dropped, and the facility rebranded as simply 'Terminal 2'.

The first incarnation of Flybe moved its operations across from Terminal 1, and Birmingham became the firm's largest base until its undignified collapse on March 5, 2020. At the time, Flybe flew to 24 destinations, making up around 30% of BHX's scheduled capacity.

Over the years, there have been other notable tenant airlines:

• Air France and its Brit Air subsidiary returned to Terminal 2 on October 31, 2010, following the launch of a codeshare agreement with Flybe for services to Paris/Charles de Gaulle and Lyon. The carrier was a former resident until moving its operations along with KLM to Terminal 1 on March 11, 2009. ➘

The Eurohub moniker was eventually dropped, and the facility rebranded as simply 'Terminal 2' *Key Collection*

In 2001, Eurohub celebrated its tenth birthday, and since opening, the terminal had welcomed 17.85 million passengers, and there had been approximately 355,500 aircraft movements *Key Collection*

Flybe moved its operations over to the terminal when it took over BA Connect in 2007 and was a major user of the terminal until the airline's demise in March 2020 *AirTeamImages.com/ Derek Pedley*

- Ryanair announced its intention to open a two-aircraft base at Terminal 2 on January 15, 2008. The airline had served BHX from Dublin since 1993 and moved its operations from Terminal 1 on June 4, 2008.
- Jet2.com became the facility's latest resident when it commenced operations on March 30, 2017. For summer 2025, the airline will have 16 aircraft based at BHX, including both the Boeing 737-800 and its new Airbus A321neos, offering over 210 weekly flights.
- Other carriers that have used Eurohub/Terminal 2 and handled high numbers of passengers through the years include Loganair, Manx Airlines, Eastern Airways, Sabena/Brussels Airlines, CityJet, Aer Lingus, Swiss, Deutsche BA and TUI.

The facility today

Thanks to various internal and external alterations, Eurohub is now completely unrecognisable. In January 2010, Paul Kehoe, the airport's then CEO, announced a £13m 'One Terminal' project to merge the two terminals to "improve passenger flows and operational efficiency." Work began in March that year, and the huge task was completed on May 13, 2011.

American dreams

On April 1, 1993, British Airways reinstated a transatlantic link from Birmingham to New York/JFK, last served by BOAC in 1973. Initially operated by a Boeing 767-300ER, the service was later extended to Toronto. Following a drop in demand, the flight was downgraded to a narrowbody 757 in January 1995 before being withdrawn completely in October 1998.

When American Airlines became one of the founding members of the oneworld alliance along with British Airways in 1999, they moved their daily Chicago/O'Hare service to Eurohub. The flight, then operated by a 767-300ER, was sadly removed from the schedules in October 2002 following the September 11 terror attacks. Optimism following its return in May 2015 – with direct links to New York – was short-lived, as the Dallas-based carrier pulled out of the Midlands gateway once again in January 2017.

When American Airlines became one of the founding members of the oneworld alliance along with BA in 1999, they moved their daily Chicago/O'Hare service to Eurohub *Key Collection*

Considerable changes were made to the internal layout, including a larger and more streamlined centralised security area. There were also updates to both landslide and airside retail units and a spacious new 20,000sq ft World Duty Free store that is 50% larger than the previous offering. The improvements increased BHX's capacity to 18 million passengers per year.

Speaking at the time, Kehoe said, "Most airports under ten million passengers do not need two terminals with two security search areas, two retail and catering offers, and split-site operations. We therefore embarked on this project to make the operation more efficient, to create a better passenger experience, and to offer a facility that is easy to get through.

"Combining the two terminals into one has been a very challenging redevelopment, with many complicated activities taking place in a 24-hour live operation. A great deal of planning, partnerships and hard work by everyone involved has produced this first-class facility, on programme, on time, and with minimal passenger disruption."

The work also coincided with the dropping of 'International' from the West Midland site's title to become simply 'Birmingham Airport.'

Future prospects

In 2018, Birmingham unveiled a new masterplan to take the facility up to 2030, with Eurohub now known as the 'South Terminal'. Building work was suspended in May 2020 due to COVID-19 but has since recommenced, and various developments and internal reconfigurations have taken place, further integrating the two terminals.

This has included a £10.6m spend in infrastructure upgrades to ensure a smoother and more efficient experience for passengers. Works have included the addition of new baggage carousels and expanded immigration facilities.

In January 2025, Solihull Council approved an increase in night flights at the facility, aiming to increase annual passenger numbers to 18 million by 2033. Last year, the airport handled 13 million passengers, and it is forecast to see 13.8 million pass through this year.

There is also the planned integration with the controversial High Speed 2 (HS2) railway line, bringing the airport within 32 minutes of travel time to the capital. The airport will be served by Birmingham Interchange station, with an Automated People Mover (APM) carrying up to 2,100 passengers per hour between the terminal and the station.

As the airport looks to the next exciting chapter in its history, it's clear that Eurohub played a pivotal role in the growth of Birmingham Airport. As the world's first purpose-built hub terminal, it broke the mould for airport design and operations, with its blueprint being reused at new facilities worldwide. ✈

The Millennium Link connected the two terminals, allowing easy access between the buildings
Key Collection

The terminal building in 1999 *Key Collection*

FEATURE
EYW
KEY WEST
UNITED STATES
airports of the world

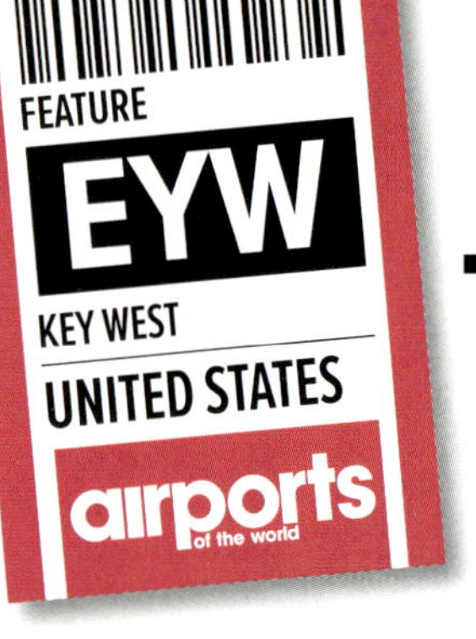

The keys to Key West

Chris Sloan heads to the far end of the Florida Keys to report on the rationale, build and opening of Concourse A at Key West International Airport

At the western tip of the Florida Keys archipelago, just 90 miles north of Cuba, lies the world-famous paradise of Key West. The airport was anything but, although its 'from the tarmac' boarding was undeniably charming, even for non-aviation enthusiasts. Conversely, the diminutive, over-crowded and windowless 1957 concourse had long outlived its sell-by date.

That bygone era ended at 0700hrs on Monday, April 14, with the pushback of Delta Air Lines flight DL1072 to Atlanta/Hartsfield-Jackson, as Key West International Airport's new Concourse A opened for its soft launch. Rather than enduring scorching heat or soaking storms, passengers boarded from the gleaming, ultra-modern 48,802sq ft edifice onto the Airbus A319 via one of eight air-conditioned airbridges – the first ever in the Florida Keys. "You lucky people are on the very first flight out of the new airport, on the first jet bridge out of Key West," announced Delta agent and local celebrity Mitch Jones. Weary tourists, some sunburnt, some a little hungover, all mostly subdued at the end of their holiday applauded and cheered, regardless of the early hour.

First impressions

The sleek new Concourse A extracted wide eyes and smiles from its first passengers, drawing a wow factor more akin to a major hub than a small airport on a tropical island. The centrepiece is a curtain of 446 electrochromic glass panels that can switch between transparent and opaque states in response to an electrical voltage that moderates the blistering sun. With the

> "After 68 years, the lights went down on the old concourse after a Sunday night American Airlines arrival from Miami"

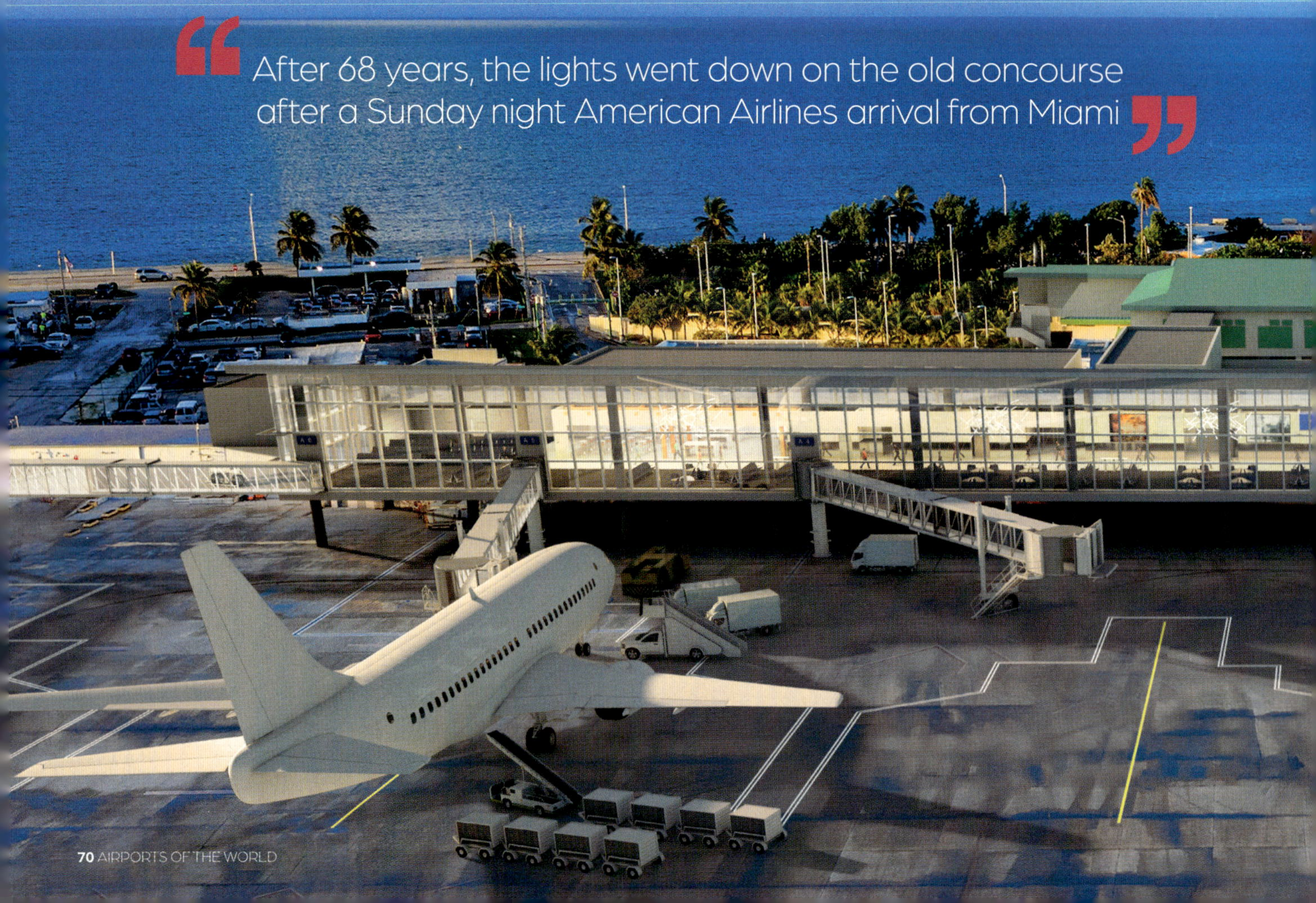

How Concourse A was imagined, before it was built *Monroe County Airports*

Keys located in a hurricane zone, the glass is rated to withstand 200mph winds. A pattern of dots on the glass spaced at two-inch intervals makes planespotting for the birds, but also prevents those same feathered aviators from seeing their reflection and crashing beak-first into the windows. Airport officials and architects worked with local wildlife preservation groups to review their concerns and gain approval for the pattern. The natural light pouring into the building with its vaulted ceilings projects a sense of calm and connection with nature, while suspended twisted glass fixtures and propeller-inspired ceiling fans complete the canopy.

Modern airport amenities abound at the new Key West, including large common-use gates with comfortable seating, ensuring everyone has a place to sit and many featuring AC electrical and USB phone chargers. Such luxuries are a considerable upgrade from the old gates where finding a seat was often futile. Coral blue carpet, evocative of the island's reef-protected ocean waters, and terrazzo cover the floor, while stand-up tables, now en vogue at major airports, have also found their way here. The washrooms, which used to have longer queues than Disney World, are plentiful, spacious, and beautifully appointed with marble finishes and automated fixtures – a welcome addition for those partaking in one last beverage before departure.

Concourse A encompasses the Southern Point bar, a grab-and-go convenience market and three

As the building rose from its foundations, repurposed shipping containers became tunnels through the construction zone, leading from the gates to the ramp
Chris Sloan

restaurants – the most well-known being The Conch Flyer, a local institution. The 'Flyer' dates back to the 1970s and the golden days of Keys aviation, when DC-3s still dotted the ramp. Airline memorabilia adorns the walls, particularly for the late Pan Am which operated its inaugural service – also America's first international flight – to Havana from Key West back in 1927.

Some people are resistant to change, bemoaning the loss of the romance of walking across the ramp, relishing the tropical breezes and salt air. Others criticise its imposing scale and modern architecture that lacks any island vibe as out of step for a destination that prides itself on a historic nautical look. "It's nice, but just looks like any other modern airport," noted one passenger. Monroe County's highly regarded art in public places committee is gearing up to install commissioned local art to soften the work-in-progress minimalist, sterile look.

Others fear the new facility will bring a greater influx of tourists into a one-by four-mile island that already attracts over a million tourists annually. The airport catchment area extends for 40 miles

Above: **The airport continued to operate as normal during the construction of Concourse A**
Key West International Airport

Above middle: **Manufactured by ThyssenKrupp, the L-shaped airbridge at Gate 8 may be the longest of its kind anywhere in the United States**
Key West International Airport/Katie Atkins

into the middle Florida Keys and Marathon Airport, which lost its commercial air service years ago, although there are rumours of American Eagle returning. However, most comments are positive and Concourse A, at almost seven times the size of the previous downtrodden facility it replaced, is merely catching up with demand. The number of gates and apron positions are unchanged.

In 2009, the 1957 terminal was extended with the addition of a second building located above the car park and connected by a bridge spanning the road below. It increased the floor space from 700sq ft to 7,000sq ft and the seating from 80 to 400 and remains unchanged. The scale and aesthetics of the McCoy building, as it's known, is more in character with the island's architecture.

The Conch Republic

Key West, for better and for worse, has experienced a tourism boom and upmarket shift into a premium and premium-priced destination, particularly since the COVID-19 pandemic. According to US Department of Transportation statistics, passenger numbers rocketed from 969,069 in 2019 to 1,449,649 in 2024. In percentage

> " There's still a perception that the airport only attracts regional propeller aircraft, yet Airbus A319s, Boeing 737-700s and Embraer E175s dominate the ramp "

The 1957 terminal in the 1990s, before the 2009 expansion
Monroe County Library Collection

terms, the facility has been coping with one of the fastest growth rates of any US airport, for which the old terminal was woefully ill-equipped.

Local islanders account for just 4% of the scheduled passenger traffic, with the rest made up entirely of visitors. While 24% of overnight visitors fly directly into the airport, 21% opt to fly into Miami and drive a rental car down

Above: The soft launch of Concourse A as the sun broke over the distant horizon *Chris Sloan*

Left: A new era in aviation begins at the western end of the Florida Keys *Key West International Airport*

the world-famous Overseas Highway, comprising 41 islands connected by 40 bridges. According to a 2024 Tourist Development Council commissioned report, 42% of people arrive by personal and rental vehicle. Diverting more leisure-based air traffic into Key West offers a growth opportunity for the airport, potentially reducing the volume of cars on the narrow and often crowded Overseas Highway. Since 2019, the facility has welcomed three new airlines, seen an 80% increase in available seats and witnessed the opening of seven new nonstop routes.

Amidst the recent meteoric growth, there's still a perception that the airport only attracts regional propeller aircraft, yet Airbus A319s, Boeing 737-700s and Embraer E175s dominate the ramp. Since Silver Airways ceased flying in June, scheduled turboprop flights have vanished entirely. With 19 nonstop services to destinations as far afield as Boston/Logan, Chicago/O'Hare, Dallas/Fort Worth, New York/La Guardia and Atlanta/Hartsfield-Jackson, the facility offers up

to 200 departures a week during peak times, according to Cirium research.

Seven carriers serve the airport, with American Airlines and its wholly-owned regional operator Envoy leading the market share at 40%. Delta Air Lines and United Airlines vie for second and third place, with Allegiant Air occupying best of the rest. Southwest Airlines pulled out of the market in 2013 after its merger with AirTran, who originally operated services to Atlanta and Tampa. The short 5,076ft runway 09/27 precludes low-cost carriers like Spirit Airlines and Frontier Airlines from operating as their A320neos would have to take a payload penalty.

Concourse A (there isn't a B) isn't a catalyst for more flights, but Key West continues to attract new airlines. Breeze Airways became the first new carrier to inaugurate a service at the new terminal when it landed on June 12, 2025. Its point-to-point model suggests significant new route opportunities should the initial Orlando/International and Tampa Bay routes be successful. Breeze and ↘

IATA Code:	EYW
ICAO Code:	KEYW
Location:	24° 33′ 22″ N, 81° 45′ 34″ W
Elevation:	3ft
Runway:	09/27 5,076 x 100ft
Website:	https://eyw.com/

JetBlue Airways fly Airbus A220-300s into Key West, an aircraft optimised for greater range from shorter runways. Before the pandemic, Air Canada looked closely at Key West, which already has US Customs Border and Protection facilities used by executive and cargo planes. With the tumult over Donald Trump's tariffs and tail-off of Canadian tourism, these plans have been shelved again.

From the ground up

The $100m airport development is the most expensive project in the history of Monroe County and was approved by the Board of County Commissioners in October 2021 as the post-COVID-19 travel boom peaked. Monroe County selected a joint-venture firm as lead contractors: Kendall, Florida-based NV2A Gulf and locally based Keystar Construction. Groundbreaking took place in November 2022, and as the building rose from its foundations, the airport installed repurposed shipping containers to act as tunnels under the construction zone from the gates to the ramp. Topping out of the new structure occurred on June 4, 2024.

Three months later, the first of eight all-glass airbridges arrived, making front page news in Key West. Manufactured by Germany's ThyssenKrupp, they are

still something of a rarity in the US, and the L-shaped airbridge at Gate 8 may be the longest of its kind in America. A late addition to the master plan after construction had begun, it has two segments because it will eventually connect to the airport's US Customs and Border Protection building and futureproof the airport for any resumption of international flights. The $5m airbridge resulted from an extra grant from the Federal Aviation Administration (FAA). Allegiant will be its main occupant, enjoying the most expansive views of the airfield from its location at the eastern end of Concourse A.

The soft opening took place six months later than the original target date, although the project isn't suffering from the cost overruns that are notorious for programmes of this scale. Richard Strickland, Monroe County's director of

airports, stated: "Are we still in budget in terms of all change orders that have been approved? We're within that budget, but have we gone over the original budget? Absolutely, because you have a change order", noting the addition of the $5m Gate 8.

However, local taxpayers aren't footing the bill for the new facility, as Katie Atkins, Key West Airport's communications director, made clear: "The project was completely funded by $41.34m in bond proceeds, Florida Department of Transportation grants, FAA grants, passenger facility charges (PFCs) and airport revenues. No local tax dollars were used." Enhanced user fees for airlines and increased rents and concession revenues will be used to pay back the bonds.

Strickland added: "It's not a revenue driver for the county. It's a revenue driver in terms of economic impact." In 2025, the FAA recognised Strickland as

By early on day two, almost all of the opening day glitches had been resolved, allowing passengers to relax *Chris Sloan*

A pattern of dots on the glass spaced at two-inch intervals prevents birds from crashing into the windows *Chris Sloan*

commercial service airport manager of the year, southern region.

A new dawn

During the entire build project, flight operations were not curtailed or paused and, as opening day approached, airport and airline crews worked round-the-clock installing and learning new IT systems, training for airbridge operations and navigating common-use gates – different from the old dedicated gates set-up. With a temporary certificate of occupancy in hand and a green light for its ambitious opening day, Concourse A was ready for its soft opening on April 14, 2025.

After 68 years, the lights went down on the old concourse after a Sunday night American Airlines arrival from Miami. Personnel worked through the night to make the switchover. As Strickland said: "There is no simulation to be done beforehand. All the electronics have to just switch over from downstairs to here." Overnight, workers drywalled over the old terminal entrance, redirecting passengers over the new bridge to the new Concourse A.

Monday morning was a subdued affair with no media present, except for myself, who found traversing from the 2009 McCoy building through to Concourse A without signage or public announcement to be a pleasant experience. Before dawn, the front-of-house scene was relatively calm, though crews were still installing the computer systems at Gate 1 where flight DL1072 would later depart. Concessions were limited to a grab-and-go market, which was stocking its shelves for the first time, and a portable Conch Flyer bar located in front of the still-under-construction Chili's Bar & Grill.

Opening day snags were abundant: the public address system, printers, scanners, flight information monitors (some amusingly displaying vertically), Wi-Fi and seat power were not functioning properly, if at all. It took one agent 15 minutes to dock an airbridge as passengers cheered encouragingly. Despite the glitches, all 30 flights scheduled that day departed on time and, by the second day, all of these issues, except for the Wi-Fi, were resolved.

From its opening day, Concourse A has justified its construction and the time-warp will continue. By the summer of 2026, Phase Two will usher in an enlarged arrivals hall, a brand new baggage system and a makeover of the beloved First Call Beach Bar. The 1957 terminal will be repurposed for operations offices and a new car rental facility. After restoration, Seward Johnson's iconic sculpture *New Friends* will move from its perch on the ramp above arrivals to a new home inside. At last, Key West, a 200-year-old city, can celebrate its past, yet have an impressive international gateway for its future. ✈

ON THE WATERFRONT

As Venice/Marco Polo works on its extension project, **Robert Veitch** travels to the Italian airport to meet key figures, discover its history and learn how the build is progressing

Above: **Emirates Boeing 777-31HER, A6-ENJ (c/n 35605),** landing at Venice as flight EK135 after a 5hr 52min rotation from Dubai *All images Key-Robert Veitch unless stated*

Right: **The departures board in the check-in hall highlights some of the 50 operators that use the airport**

Rising up just above the waterline of the Venetian Lagoon at the northern end of the Adriatic Sea is the floating city of Venice. Once a maritime power and a centre of commerce, it became a place of great wealth. Over time, patrons constructed ever more palatial buildings and began fostering the arts, evolving the city into a cultural hotspot encompassing music, literature, theatre, art and, more recently, film and fashion.

In February 1954, a commission decided to build a new airport for the cultural capital on marshy ground beside the lagoon, adjacent to the village of Tessera. Land reclamation began in March 1958 and, after construction of a pair of parallel 9,121ft runways and a passenger terminal, the facility opened on July 31, 1961. It was named Venice/Marco Polo after the 13th century Venetian merchant, explorer and writer. Though sited just 7ft above the waterline, it was on solid ground, unlike the city. Early passengers admired aerial views of the lagoon, city and coastline, which has continued through the decades.

In 1974, the primary runway 04R/22L was extended to 10,827ft to make the facility accessible to larger aircraft, including the Boeing 747. During the years that followed, although the original terminal was enlarged twice, it was generally viewed as a featureless structure, so the decision to start again was taken after a review in the late 1990s. The original structure remains in situ, adjacent to the old air traffic control tower at one end and the water terminal

at the other, although it is primarily used for maintenance.

The current terminal, with a vast new apron, opened in 2002 and was part of a 2030 masterplan. Architect Gian Paolo Mar was given the task of integrating it with the local architectural landscape. Inspiration was said to come from the Gaggiandre and Fondaci warehouses, two former military buildings to the southwest of the city.

The build incorporated concrete, terracotta brickwork, natural stone, marble wood, and Istrian stone for the pillars and decoration. The unique copper roofing and octagonal towers put a modern twist on the existing architecture around the lagoon. The Venetian theme flowed through the building, from the vaulted hammer beamed wooden ceiling to the dark hardwood flooring in sections of the departure lounge, with the curvature of the airbridges mirroring the canal-spanning bridges of the city. When it came to shutting down the old terminal and moving into the current one, Camillo Bozzolo, the commercial director for aviation at airport operator Societa Aeroporto di Venezia (SAVE), remarked: "Overnight, we stopped operations there and moved everything here."

Adjacent to a vast northern and eastern apron, the 645,856sq ft terminal had an official capacity of 6.5 million passengers per year when it opened. Between 2000 and 2002, in the final years of the old terminal, traffic crept up from 4.14 million to 4.22 million annually. With the new facility open, traffic surged and 2003 ended with 5.3 million passengers, a year-on-year increase of 26%. This was primarily due to the larger, more efficient terminal that offered airlines the capacity to operate bigger aircraft. Low-cost carriers moved in, including Germanwings, easyJet, Hapag-Lloyd Express, Volareweb and Deutsche BA, along with regional carrier Alpi Eagles.

By 2007, the number of passengers carried rose to 7.08 million, exceeding the hub's theoretical capacity, though numbers fell back in 2008-2011 as the global financial crisis restricted growth. At the time, Alitalia only flew domestic routes from Marco Polo, and low-cost carriers easyJet and Germanwings were joined by airBaltic, Sterling Airlines, Cimber, Jet2.com, bmibaby, Vueling, Norwegian Air Shuttle and XL Airways. Long-haul operators included Delta Air Lines, Emirates, US Airways, Air Transat and Qatar Airways.

During 2010, the facility served 6.9 million passengers and was the fifth most populous airport in Italy after Rome/Fiumicino, Milan/Malpensa, Milan/Linate and Milan/Bergamo. By 2011, 72% of passengers arrived on international flights, with the remainder coming from a slowly shrinking percentage of domestic links – the rest of the world was keen to visit with ever increasing frequency.

Terminal expansion commenced in 2013 and, in 2016, the water terminal was opened, connected to the main complex by an elevated moving walkway. Perhaps the most magnificent arrival into the city is provided by the ↘

> "The decision to start again was taken after a review in the late 1990s"

After a 12hr 44min flight from Seoul, Asiana Airlines Boeing 777-28EER, HL-7739 (c/n 29175), was attached to one of the unique octagonal towers

Alilaguna water shuttles – quite the way to make an entrance – cruising down the Grand Canal for the first time is something never to be forgotten. The following year, 2017, witnessed the completion of phase one with the opening of the 22 metre wide, 280 metre long plaza that links the 2002 terminal with the parallel split-level access roads. An arched glass gridshell roof spans the top floor – a beguiling, complex, light streaming geometry, with an unmistakable 'wow' factor.

Corrado Fischer, chief operating officer of SAVE Group, said: "In 2019, we rebuilt and renewed our runway systems, and these were the big investments – around €130m." Bozzolo explained how the runways have evolved: "Originally, all the exits were at 90°, [but] by putting in quick exit ways, you get more movements per hour."

Global design and consultancy firm One Works, who envisioned phase one, have also designed phase two, a €2bn expansion that will increase capacity to 21 million passengers per year by 2037. It will include a Schengen extension to the northwest of the terminal and a passport-control extension to the southwest of the structure, plus a new railway station to further enhance connectivity. The phase two build is underway and Bozzolo said the development is modular: "We aren't building everything together. Additional Schengen areas will be connected by a bridge, but eventually [we] will also fill that area."

Fischer explained the extensions will open in stages "because we have to catch up with the needs of the traffic",

> **The unique copper roofs and octagonal towers put a modern twist on the existing architecture around the lagoon**

some being Schengen and others being passport departures. In time "we will completely rebuild all the baggage handling systems... to be completed around 2030-2031 and, by 2037, the capacity will have increased to 21 million passengers per year."

The terminal has seven airbridges currently, but the final count could stretch to 14 when the expansion is complete. Bozzolo hinted the essence of the original airport will always remain: "Where you are sitting is this fantastic little building. We will keep

it like this, so we don't forget where we've come from."

Work is well underway on the new underground railway station, due to open in time for the 2026 Milan-Cortina Winter Olympics. Work began on the five-mile line in December 2023 and will include 2.1 miles of tunnelling and 0.33 miles of viaduct. Linked directly to the terminal by a walkway, the loop line was something the airport fought for, as Bozzolo explained: "It's a through train station. The idea is that the high-speed rail line goes through and it continues its journey [on the main line]. There are a number of stations – Milano, Brescia, Verona, Vicenza – it's the east west line, what's called corridor five, from Lyon to Budapest." Fischer noted it will complete the facility's connectivity "because we will have water, rail and rubber [road]."

Airlines and routes

At the end of 2022, Marco Polo was ranked the sixth busiest airport in Italy, with 9.3 million passengers per year, having moved ahead of Linate, but fallen behind Naples and Catania. The hub is home to a mix of low-cost and legacy airlines, offering a network that supports tourism, business and destinations to which Italians have emigrated. Fifty airlines fly from the airport, of which nine carriers operate 11 long-haul routes, and annual traffic is fairly evenly spread through all

The arched glass gridshell roof of the 280 metre long plaza

Looking out from stand 326 under leaden skies

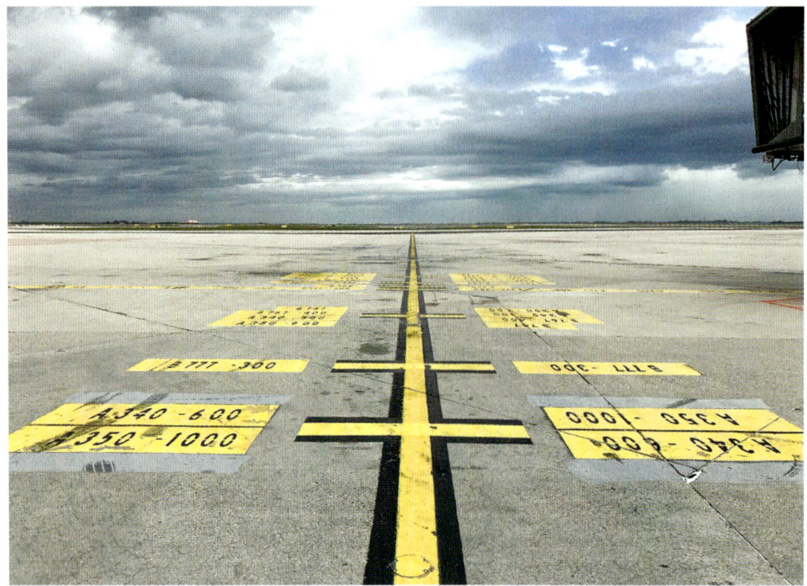

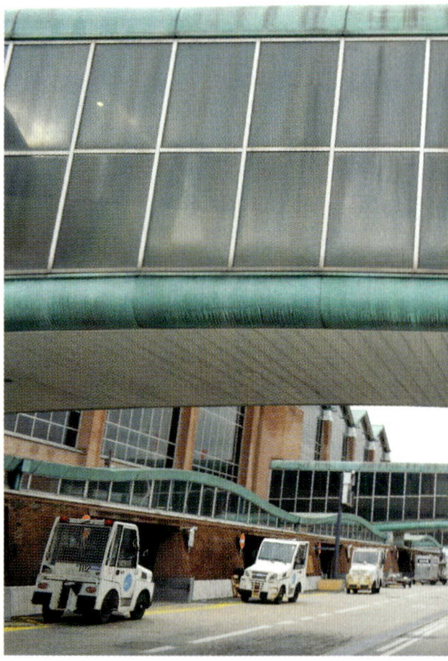

four quarters. Around 80% of current movements are international and the airport handles 2.4 million transit passengers each year.

Bozzolo said the region is home to businesses such as Luxottica (eyeglasses), Dainese (motorcycle protective equipment), Carraro (vehicle transmissions) and the Italian tanning industry that provides the automotive sector with cured leather, each in close proximity to the airport. He noted it can be "difficult to get intercontinental traffic as the third airport, [airlines] want to go to the capital first, then secondary. We're a tertiary, so we better have a pretty good business case, and that's what we usually have."

Keen to add new routes, the airport welcomed China Eastern Airlines in September 2024, operating thrice-weekly services to Shanghai/Pudong, which the airport thought particularly apt on the 700th anniversary of Marco Polo's death. Staff were "here at dawn, ready for the 6.50am arrival. We have been trying to get direct links with China for the last decade... United has announced Venice to Washington DC from May to October 2025." In addition, from June 2025, American Airlines will begin daily services from Dallas/Fort Worth.

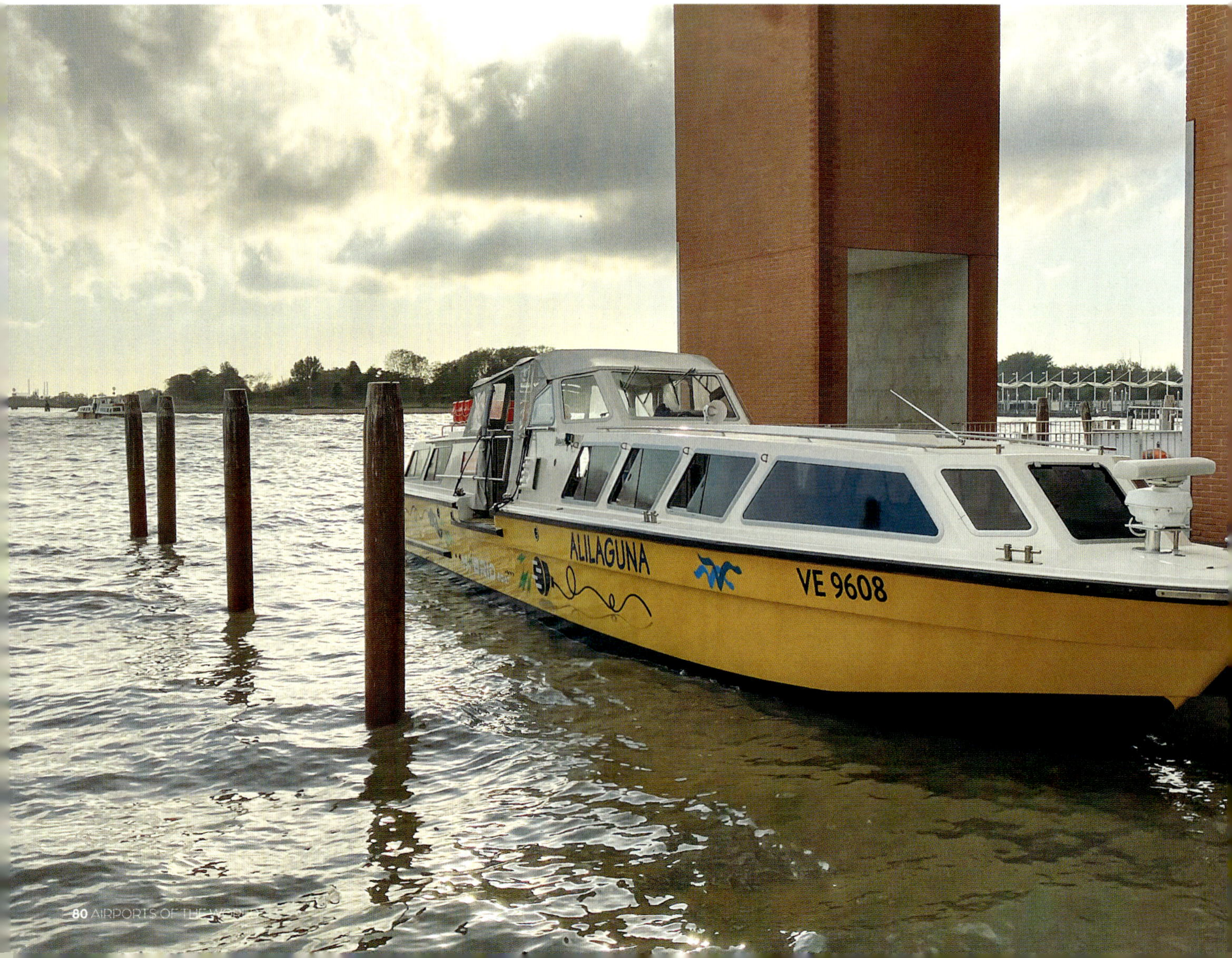

Perhaps the most magnificent arrival into the city is provided by Alilaguna water shuttles

The future

Marco Polo has been run by SAVE since 1987. It also operates Treviso, Brescia and Verona airports and is a partner in the running of Brussels/Charleroi. Fischer said: "It's a private company. The owner of all the airports in Italy is the Ministry of Transportation through its aeronautical arm. Then through tenders, they give the concession of the airports to a third

> **By 2037 the capacity will have increased to 21 million passengers per year**

company." The concession for SAVE at Marco Polo runs until 2043.

While it's difficult to see into the future, Fischer was adamant there would be no future land reclamation for further expansion: "It is impossible in the lagoon, [because] the environmental rules we are subjected to in this part of the region are very, very strict. We cannot move one single glass of water from it, it's forbidden." While the city was built on tree trunks and is slowly sinking, the airport land reclamation is on a firmer footing and safe for the future. Fischer said: "The runways are 1.2 metres higher than the medium average of the of the site."

The appeal of the hub is broader than one might imagine. Marco Polo cannot and doesn't rely on the city of Venice. While the general perception might be that the vast majority of arriving passengers head for the city, Fischer revealed that recent studies by the airport indicated that "roughly 40% of people landing in Venice go to Venice, and the other 60% don't. This is the northeast region, so we get people from Croatia, Slovenia, Austria, from the southern Veneto area – Bologna, from Trentino to Adige – it's a very big catchment area", totalling nine to ten million people within a two-hour drive.

Bozzolo agreed: "Ultimately the catchment area of this airport is the second richest area in Italy. We have 25% of all SMEs in Italy based in this area [and] the lowest unemployment. We have the highest GDP per capita in all of the country." He went on to suggest other cities "would give an arm to have the cultural baggage that Treviso has, or that Padua has, or that Vicenza has – except they are all outshone by Venice." ✈

Venice's aviation origins

Marco Polo is the third airport to be linked to the city of Venice, a descendant in a line that began just six years after the Wright brothers first defied gravity.

Venice/Lido or Giovanni Nicelli Airport is located at the northern tip of a seven-mile-long barrier island that separates the lagoon from the Adriatic – a ten-minute boat ride from the city. Aircraft first flew from a grass airstrip, sited just 13ft above sea level, in 1909 and it was later used as a World War One base. In 1926, a flight to Vienna departed from the 3,261ft runway 05/23 to become the city's first commercial service. The terminal was inaugurated on February 4, 1935, and is regarded as a perfectly preserved, still functioning example of 1930s architecture. It remained the gateway to Venice until 1953 when services transferred to Treviso and Lido was limited to domestic flights, though it remains the oldest commercial airport in Italy.

Located 19 miles from Venice, Lido's demise proved Treviso's gain. The latter was initially developed in the 1930s, but opened up to international traffic from 1953 with the construction of a small passenger terminal. With the elevation of Marco Polo to primary facility status in recent decades, Treviso has become the preserve of low-cost carriers and home to Wizz Air and Ryanair

FEATURE
SOU
SOUTHAMPTON
UNITED KINGDOM
airports
of the world
SUPER
SIZING
SOUTHAMPTON
easyJet
easyJet
KLM
KLM cityhopper
PH-EXG
swissport

As air travel spluttered to a stop at the start of the COVID-19 pandemic, the downturn at Southampton Airport was more akin to an abrupt halt. While other airports around the world pivoted into survival mode, Southampton was an outlier and the fight for survival commenced before the footfall plummeted.

The airport had a long association with Jersey European Airways, the initial incarnation of regional carrier Flybe. Given its proximity to the Channel Islands, it's not surprising the airport had a strong partnership with the airline. The collaboration blossomed in 2003, the year after the Flybe rebrand, resulting in a three-fold increase in the number of routes served and passengers flown, over the following four years. The carrier offered a diverse range of routes, ranging from short hops to Manchester to more distant seasonal destinations such as Faro. In a stroke of misfortune, this partnership ended on March 5, 2020, when Flybe ceased operations and was placed into administration. Overnight 90% of Southampton's flights evaporated, and this south coast gateway was propelled into recovery mode, and what proved to be one of its darkest hours.

Groundbreaking days

Amid this poignant and challenging episode in history lies a rich tapestry of heritage that spans more than a century. Sqn Ldr Edwin Rowland Moon, a distinguished military aviator, made history in 1910 by taking flight from the meadows at North Stoneham Farm in his single-seat, self-built and self-designed Moonbeam II aircraft. During World War One, the aerodrome was transferred to the US Navy Air Service and became known as NAS Eastleigh. On March 5, 1936, aircraft manufacturer Supermarine conducted the first test flight of a Spitfire prototype from what was now named RAF Southampton. Its factory in nearby Woolston produced hundreds of Spitfires over the following years.

After peace came, Southampton quickly established commercial services and during the 1950s as traffic grew, the airfield served as a vital link between the south coast, Channel Islands, and France. Operator Silver City Airways frequently used iconic aircraft like the Bristol Type 170 Freighter to provide a unique car ferry service to Cherbourg on the French coast. While the airport steadily expanded over the following decades, it wasn't until the 1990s that it began to resemble the look of today. In 1990, the British Airports Authority (BAA) purchased the facility and announced a £27m investment for the complete redevelopment of the airport. During the following year, the airport was renamed Southampton International Airport and a new terminal was opened, which is still in use today. AGS Airports acquired the airport in 2014 after BAA restructured its airport portfolio in response to concerns about its perceived monopoly at the time. While selling Southampton was not a prerequisite, BAA elected to solely focus on Heathrow.

Extending the runway

Statistics from the Civil Aviation Authority (CAA) paint a sobering picture of Flybe's demise on the airport. Passenger throughput plummeted by 83% from 2019 to 2020, which was 8% worse

than the national average. In terms of aircraft movements, there was a 70% year-on-year decrease, compared to a national average of 54%. The old adage of 'putting all your eggs in one basket' underscored the gravity of the situation at Southampton. Mark Beveridge, interim operations director provided an update on the changing fortunes at Southampton, and the journey back to prosperity.

Even before the pandemic, it was apparent that Southampton's runway's length was a barrier to future growth. While the airport was no stranger to turboprops and regional jets of the Embraer variety, attracting operators with larger airframes such as the Boeing 737 and the Airbus A320 Family proved more of a challenge. In order to open the door to welcome new carriers operating larger aircraft, planning permission for a 164m runway extension was lodged in November 2019. AGS Airports focused on containing any expansion within the confines of the existing perimeter. Although 164m might not seem substantial, it does enable larger aircraft to provide connectivity to the same variety of routes already served, in preference to developing new routes to more distant destinations. Beveridge explained the aim is to strive to develop capacity on routes within a 1,000nm radius. So while popular leisure destinations in the southwest Mediterranean will be easily accessible,

reaching more distant destinations such as the Greek Islands will remain more of a challenge.

As with any big airport infrastructure project, the local community expressed both support and opposition. Opponents were worried about the widespread use of larger aircraft and increased noise levels. After a series of judgments and appeals, the process came to a close in August 2022, when the Court of Appeal finally approved the expansion project. Construction work took place at night between 11pm and 6.30am when the airport was closed, as Beveridge explained: "The main challenge was ensuring we maintained an operational runway throughout the construction phase, and this meant all of the groundwork was carried out at night before handing back a safe and compliant runway every morning."

The night curfew remains in place after the runway works. In tandem with the extended runway, the long-stay car

> **We want to deliver an airport that this region can be proud of and support, and the runway extension will be a great asset**

park was developed to accommodate increased passenger numbers. The extended 1,887m runway became operational on August 15, 2023, and a celebratory opening ceremony took place on September 21 with a departing Spitfire providing a fitting nod to history.

Changing fortunes

Upgrading airport infrastructure is an expensive endeavour, and although Beveridge bypassed the opportunity to assure passengers and airlines that the cost of the project would not be passed onto them, he was keen to state: "Our runway extension was completed on time and on budget."

Building new infrastructure is one thing, but enticing airlines to utilise it is an altogether separate challenge. EasyJet launched a short-lived pre-pandemic sojourn to Geneva in December 2017, which has now been reactivated. The low-cost carrier has broadened its network, adding Belfast International and Glasgow on October 29 and November 2, 2023. Turning to the more lucrative summer season, the carrier offers connections to Alicante, Faro, and Palma de Mallorca. Beveridge described the return of easyJet as an example of "early success".

In addition, long-standing resident airline KLM added a third daily flight to Amsterdam using its Embraer fleet, operated by its Cityhopper subsidiary. Aurigny Air Services and Blue Islands maintain those traditional links to the Channel Islands. With the runway extension now operational, it remains to be seen how lucrative it will prove to be. Statistics from the CAA for December 2023, typically one of the busiest winter months, revealed some encouraging news. Passenger throughput increased by 13% year on year, yet the number of movements rose only 3% during the same period. The sharper rise in passenger numbers against the smaller increase in aircraft movements does indicate more travellers per aircraft. That may be an inkling of evidence to suggest there is demand for mainstream narrowbody aircraft, such as the Boeing 737 and Airbus A320 Family.

Future plans

Reconstruction is not just confined to the ground, as the airspace around the airport is in the process of being restructured. The CAA is overseeing a feasibility study to enhance efficiency in the southeast, and airspace around Southampton could potentially benefit from exploiting more advanced flight deck technology. With modern aircraft capable of following precise satellite-guided trajectories, the airport has expressed an intent to implement departure routes reliant on satellite navigation, rather than pilots adhering to navigation instructions relayed from air traffic control, as is currently the case.

Much work is being done to reduce the noise and carbon footprint that landing aircraft generate. Feasibility studies are exploring the possibility of using satellite navigation to allow aircraft to fly their initial approach over Southampton Water, and align with the northerly runway 02, much later than is currently possible. Aircraft landing on the southerly runway 20 often need to be kept at higher than optimum altitudes due to the design of controlled airspace. This often leads to regular use of what is jocularly referred to as the 'Winchester Orbit' – an extended route flown around the Hampshire town to allow flight crews to descend and re-establish the optimum descent path. Installing additional portions of controlled airspace could provide air traffic controllers with more protected airspace to work with, enabling aircraft to fly more direct arrival routes and significantly reduce emissions. Airspace restructuring is expected be activated in 2027 at the earliest.

In its 2018 draft masterplan, Southampton airport declared terminal expansion would go hand in hand with runway expansion. With larger aircraft now funnelling more people through the existing terminal, passengers could be forgiven for thinking this structure is in the spotlight, though Beveridge suggested an intriguing 'wait and see' approach. The airport is expected to rebound to pre-COVID-19 passenger levels during 2025 or 2026, prompting a likely assessment of terminal infrastructure in the near future.

Beveridge handed over responsibility at Southampton to incoming operations director Gavin Williams on February 26, 2024. Williams moved to AGS Airports from Manchester Airports Group. Beveridge will remain in his role as operations director at Aberdeen Airport (with AGS Airports), a position he held in tandem with his post at Southampton. Reflecting on his brief tenure in Hampshire, he expressed optimism for the future saying: "We want to deliver an airport that this region can be proud of and support, and the runway extension will be a great asset." ✈

Mark Beveridge (left) celebrates the inauguration of easyJet services to Belfast and Glasgow, which commenced late in 2023 *easyJet*

Southampton's landside area

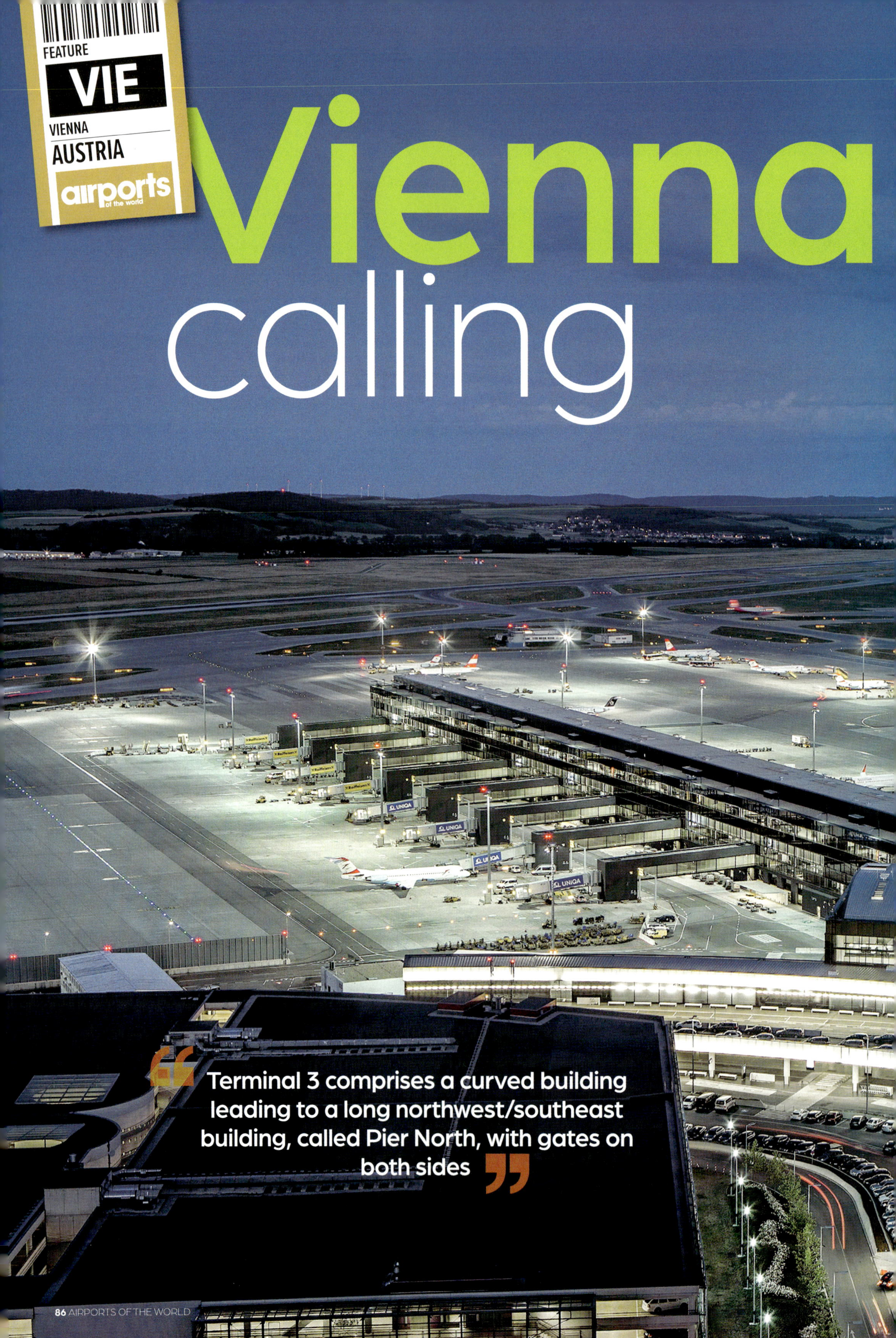

Vienna
calling

Vienna's first airport opened in June 1912 at Aspern, to the northeast of the Danube, which was one of the busiest airfields in Europe until the outbreak of World War One. Alongside its military use, it became the home of the Austrian Aero-Club (Österreichischer Aero-Club, OeAC). But the development of another airfield at Schwechat and the transfer of airline services to the new facility led to the closure of Aspern in 1977, after which it was repurposed for industry and as a vehicle testing facility.

Schwechat was originally used by Heinkel for military aircraft design and construction, and had a grass runway, 10/28. The site opened in 1938 and because of its strategic importance was bombed in World War Two and badly damaged by the time it was taken over by the British in 1945. As RAF Schwechat, the facilities were rapidly restored and commercial services operated by British European Airways (BEA) commenced in April 1952. The airfield was handed over to the newly formed Vienna Airport Authority (Wiener Flughafenbetriebsgesellschaft) in 1954, replacing Aspern as Austria's principal aerodrome. During the first full year under new ownership it handled 64,211 passengers and became a convenient gateway, linking Europe to the Soviet Bloc and the USSR. With many visiting pilots unable to speak English, it was common for radio communications to be conducted in Russian. A major expansion project started in 1959, when the single runway was lengthened to 9,843ft. A new single-storey terminal, known as Aircourt (Flughof), opened the following year, and it still forms part of the current airport infrastructure.

Further development saw airbridge-equipped gates added as part of the Pier East project in 1988. During 1992, ⬇

Pier North and the central terminal building at dusk
Flughafen Wien/ Roman Boensch

Terminal 1 opened, followed a year later by a shopping plaza in the transit area between the B, C and D gates. In 1996, Pier West, with 12 airbridges, was built and a new arrivals hall and additional check-in facilities were added.

Since the turn of the millennium, Vienna benefited from growth in low-cost travel and throughput almost doubled to 19.7 million passengers in the ten years to 2008. Passenger numbers continued to rise, increasing by 15% to reach 24.4 million passengers by 2017, then 31.7 million by the end of 2024.

Aircraft can be seen as passengers complete check-in formalities *Flughafen Wien*

At the crossroads

Austria is located at the geographical centre of the European Union and its position makes Vienna International Airport (Flughafen Wien) a strategically important hub for connecting the western and eastern halves of the continent. It's also well placed to support transfers to destinations in North America, Asia and the Middle East. The airfield is 18km southeast of Vienna and only 57km west of Bratislava, the capital of neighbouring Slovakia, enabling it to provide air transport services to residents of, and visitors to, both countries.

The biggest and busiest airport in Austria, Vienna is the base for Austrian Airlines, although low-cost carriers Ryanair and Wizz Air also maintain a significant presence. It can handle widebodies, including the Airbus A380 operated by Emirates, and has a dense network of European destinations as well as long-haul flights. There were 234,138 aircraft movements in 2024,

> "Austria is located at the geographical centre of the European Union and its position makes Vienna International Airport a strategically important hub"

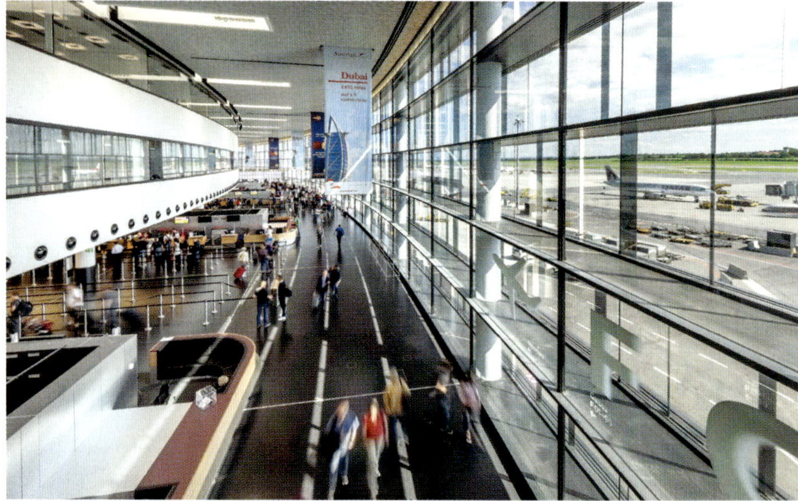

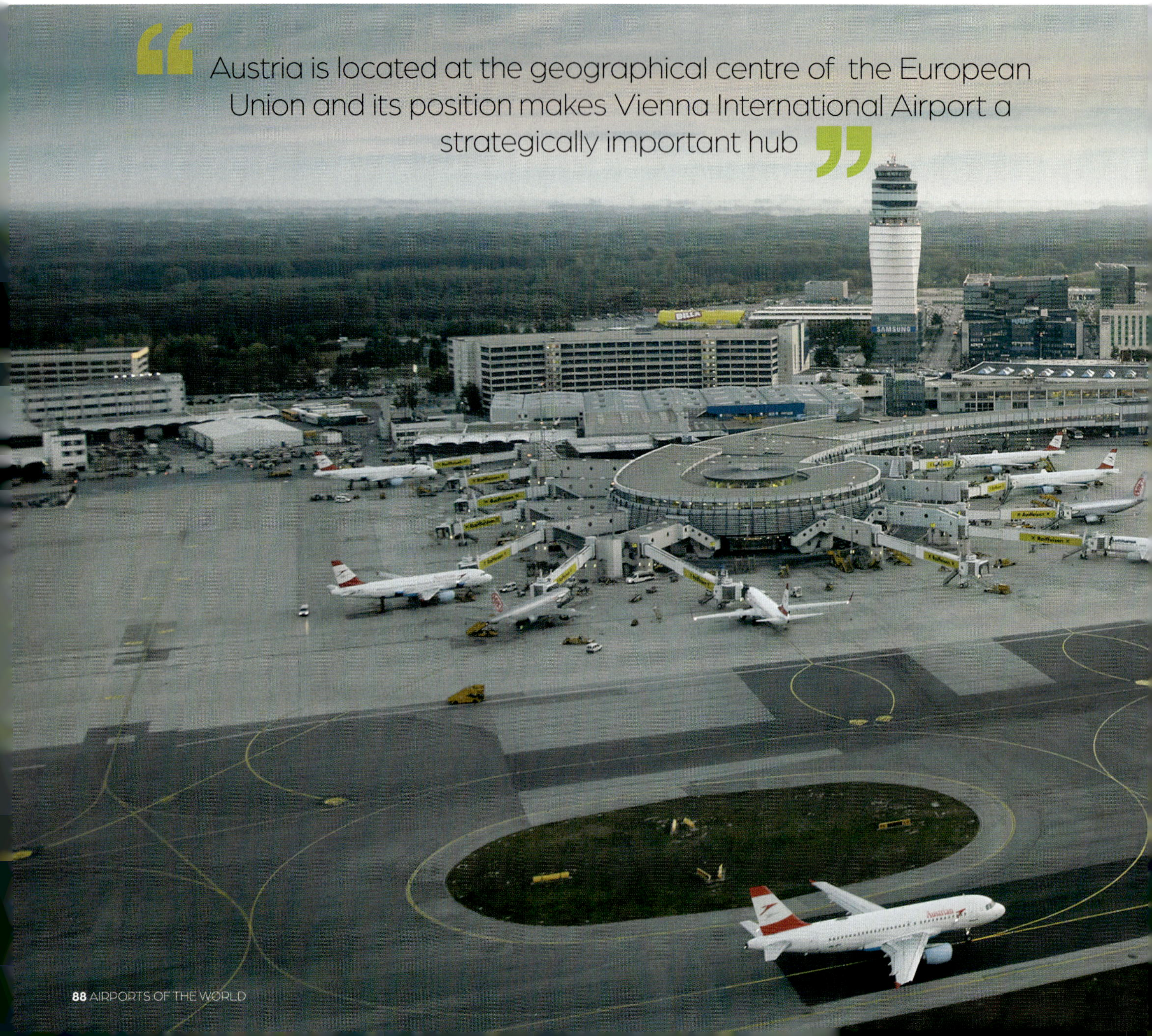

A view (L-R) from airside with Pier West, Pier East and Pier North in the foreground *Flughafen Wien*

less than the absolute peak of 292,740 in 2009, but maybe indicative of larger capacity aircraft and a higher load factor, considering passenger numbers have climbed by 12 million during the same period.

Central terminal area

There are effectively four terminals in the central area – 1, 1A, 2 and 3 – although Terminal 2 has been converted into a security screening area leading to concourse C and D on the departures level, and an improved baggage reclaim area on the arrivals level.

Terminal 1 is used by budget carriers such as Eurowings, Norwegian Air Shuttle, Ryanair and Wizz Air, plus oneworld members Aer Lingus, British Airways, Finnair and Iberia. It is also a home for SkyTeam carriers Air France, KLM Royal Dutch Airlines, Saudia and other airlines such as Air Algerie, Air Serbia, AJet, Azerbaijan Airlines, KM Malta, Kuwait Airlines, People's and Turkish Airlines. The building uses most of the floorspace of the previous Aircourt (Flughof) ➔

Vienna is the home hub of Austrian Airlines and its fleet of 68 aircraft
Austrian Airlines/ Florian Schmidt

Left: The area between the piers affords panoramic views of the aprons
Flughafen Wien

Schengen routes. It's not widely apparent, but Concourse D and the G gates are connected airside by lifts or stairs and a walkway located high above the main atrium of Terminal 3. Inbound passengers passing through any of the terminals are funnelled into a central arrivals hall on the ground floor of T3, below the departures area.

All the terminals are adjacent to the airport railway station, located underground and linked by a short walk. The nonstop City Airport Train (CAT) connects with Wien Mitte station in 16 minutes, and offers the option of a city centre check-in for a number of airlines. Other services connect to the magnificent Wien Hauptbahnhof, which opened in 2014. Coach operators based at the airport offer city connections further afield.

Around the airfield

A little further out on the airfield, Austrian Airlines' maintenance, repair and overhaul (MRO) facility occupies a site to the west of the terminal area. Here, Austrian Technik uses three hangars and employs around 800 technicians

Above: **Korean Air Cargo's 747 freighters are regular visitors from Seoul/Incheon** *Flughafen Wien*

Right: **There are 14 baggage collection carousels, with 11 of them located in Terminal 3 and the rest in what used to be the arrivals area of Terminal 2** *Key-Robert Veitch*

building and occupies the western part of the central terminal complex.

The adjacent **Terminal 1A** is used by low-cost operators Air Arabia, easyJet, Jet2.com, Pegasus Airlines, Transavia and Vueling, plus leisure carriers Condor, Corendon Airlines and Mavi Gök. It also houses Air Albania, Air Cairo, China Airlines, Freebird Airlines, Georgian Airways, Nesma Airlines, Nile Air, Nouvelair, Red Sea Airlines, Sky Express, Smartwings, Sun Express and TUS Airways.

Airside, Concourse B – with gates B22 to B42 (bus boarding) – is used for Schengen destinations. Concourse C, also known as Pier West, has 12 airbridges and is used for Schengen destinations, with gates C31 to C42 (airbridges), C21 to C24 (below) and C71 to C75 (buses). Concourse D, also known as Pier East and at one time Concourse A, has seven airbridges and is used for non-Schengen destinations. With a shared passport control at the entrance leading to gates D21 to D29 (airbridges), D31 to D36 (buses) and D61 to D70 (buses).

Terminal 3 is to the east of the central complex, on the left-hand side when arriving by road. Known as the Skylink terminal during construction, it comprises a curved building leading to a long northwest/southeast building called Pier North with gates on both sides. Opened on June 5, 2012, it's referred to as the Austrian Star Alliance Terminal, as it's used by Austrian Airlines and its Lufthansa Group partners Brussels Airlines, Lufthansa and Swiss International Air Lines. Fellow Star Alliance members Aegean Airlines, Air Canada, Air China, Air India, All Nippon Airways, Croatia Airlines, EgyptAir, Ethiopian Airlines, EVA Air, LOT Polish Airlines and TAP Air Portugal are also based here. Other airlines operating from it are airBaltic, El Al, Emirates, Etihad Airways, Hainan Airlines, Korean Air, Luxair, Qatar Airways and Tunisair.

Almost 130 check-in/bag drop counters on the first floor drive travellers through to Pier North, which has 17 airbridges. Gates F01 to 37 on level 1 are for Schengen destinations, with G01 to 37 on level 3 for non-

Some airlines offer a city centre check-in at the CAT concourse at Wien-Mitte railway station *Key-Robert Veitch*

A huge video screen adorns the wall in the arrivals area of Terminal 3 *Key-Robert Veitch*

and administrative staff. It provides line and base maintenance up to C-checks, engineering services, technical training and storage for the carrier's fleet. It also conducts third-party work on other airliners as well as supporting business aircraft through a separate division, Austrian Technik Executive Services (ATES).

As the needs of the airport grew, its single main runway 11/29 was extended – first to 3,000m in 1959 and more recently to 3,500m. By 1962, increasing passenger throughput led to an application to the Austrian transport ministry to build a second runway. But, owing to objections from conservationists, and lengthy public inquiries, construction of the 3,600m runway 16/34 did not begin for another

Pretty maids all in a row and clearly visible from the 358ft air traffic control tower, which opened in 2006 *Austrian Airlines/Michelle Pauty*

ten years. Today, aircraft are still subject to planning constraints and noise abatement procedures, requiring departures to turn left when departing on runway 29 or right from runway 34 shortly after take-off to avoid the urban areas of Vienna. There are a similar procedures for arrivals on runways 11 and 16, as well as night time restrictions.

A third runway – planned to be 3,680m in length will be sited 2.4km south of and parallel to 11/29, enabling independent and simultaneous operation and with no restrictions on landing or take-off paths. The Austrian Federal Administrative Court ruled in favour of the runway on March 28, 2018. The project, which has yet to be given a start date, will include a new taxiway network linking it to the terminals.

The check-in area at Terminal 1 *Key-Robert Veitch*

Gates G01 to 37 on level 3 of Pier North at Terminal 3 are for non-Schengen destinations
Key-Robert Veitch

Commercial traffic

The 2014 introduction of A380s on Emirates flights to Dubai represents only a portion of the developing traffic between Vienna and the Middle East, the Gulf region, India and Far East.

Austrian Airlines links its base with Amman, Cairo and Tel Aviv, as well as Tehran in Iran and Erbil in Iraq. Further afield, it flies to Bangkok, Shanghai/Pudong, Tbilisi and Tokyo/Narita, plus holiday destinations such as Gran Canaria, Marrakesh, and Mauritius. North American routes are flown to Boston, Chicago, New York/Newark, New York/JFK, Montreal and Washington, with seasonal offerings including Cancun, Los Angeles, Malé and Rovaniemi.

Emirates, Arkia, EgyptAir, El Al and Qatar Airways all provide links to burgeoning markets in the Middle East,

while Air India, Air China, China Airways, Ethiopian Airlines, EVA Air and Korean Air serve destinations further east. To the west, Austrian Airlines aside, there are no direct services by other carriers to North America. Closer to home, most major European carriers serve the airport, but a number of smaller airlines not widely seen across the continent also offer links, including Air Serbia (ATR 72-600), Electra Airways (A320 Family), Fly Lili (Airbus A319 and A320) and People's (Embraer 170).

An area to the west of the airfield is used for cargo and a UPS Boeing 767 freighter visits daily. Larger aircraft – such as the Boeing 747Fs of Cargolux, and Korean Air/Asiana Airlines along with their Boeing 777Fs, plus China Southern Airlines 777Fs – use an area north of Terminal 3. Other cargo haulers using the hub include DHL Aviation, Silk Way Airlines and Qatar Airways Cargo. During 2024, the hub handled 297,945 tonnes of cargo, the highest amount in its history.

Developing the airport

Privatised in 1992, the airport is now jointly owned by the Province of Lower Austria (20%), the City of Vienna (20%), the airport employees foundation (10%) and Airports Group Europe (44%), with the remaining 6% held by private investors. The two principal members of the Board of Flughafen Wien are chief financial officer Dr Günther Ofner and chief operating officer Julian Jäger, both of whom were appointed in 2011.

In late 2015, *Airports of the World* spoke to Jäger, who said: "Last year we handled a record number of passengers and expect 2016 to grow slightly on that figure – although we're in a challenging environment at present. Curiously, the number of aircraft movements has actually dropped, but as their size has increased, we've dealt with more people."

To emphasise the point, he explained that Emirates had upgraded its daily

VIEwing

On top of Terminal 3 is the Besucherterrasse (visitor terrace), an open-air viewing area accessed by lift from the western end of the central area close to Terminal 1. Visitors are charged €4 (children half-price) to visit the 306m terrace and are subject to a standard security check, although liquids are allowed. The facilities on the terrace are limited, but there's a vending machine next to the checkpoint and display boards along its length. It is accessible between 10am and 6pm from April to the end of October. The rooftop boasts stunning views of the aprons and both runways, although the northern side of Terminal 3, the cargo apron and executive aircraft cannot be seen.

Airside tours are available for those who want to get closer to the aircraft.

They run on most days during the summer season, from the Visitor World Terminal, costing €23.90 for adults and €17 for children. As the tour passes through the airside areas, visitors have to go through airport security and the usual array of items are prohibited, although they, along with larger bags, can be left in lockers. Participants travel on a double-decker coach with tinted windows (which may not win wide approval from photographers) and the trip takes 50 minutes. All parts of the airport are visited, including the maintenance area, executive jet apron, cargo areas and all the terminals.

Other tours are available on an ad hoc basis – check the airport website for details.

Qatar Airways 787-8 Dreamliner, A7-BCA (c/n 38319), El Al Israel Airlines 737-958ER, 4X-EHB (c/n 41553), and Air Berlin A320-214, OE-LEY (c/n 5648) at Pier East, seen from the open air terrace in 2017 *Key-Tony Dixon*

Airport Statistics

IATA Code:	VIE
ICAO Code:	LOWW
Location:	48° 06' 39" N, 16° 34' 15" E
Elevation:	183m (600ft)
Runways:	16/34 11,811 x 148ft, 11/29 11,483 x 148ft
Website:	www.viennaairport.com

service to an Airbus A380, the first of the type to operate scheduled services at Vienna: "As a result of the drop in movements, the decision on whether we go ahead with a plan for a third runway has been put back until 2025 at the earliest. We estimate that we can now handle between 35 and 40 million passengers with the current two runways, purely due to the bigger aircraft.

"Although we're the smallest hub in the Lufthansa system, we actually serve more point-to-point destinations. We have a good economic catchment area, with relatively higher salaries in the region and we're also attracting more and more tourists to this part of Austria."

The airport is open 24 hours a day, although there are some restrictions on night flights. Between 11pm and 5am, 4,000 movements per annum are permitted, although there is some leeway available – if the figure is exceeded in one year, there have to be fewer movements the next, for example.

Jäger explained that expansion of the adjacent Airport City was attracting high-tech businesses to the vicinity, and a large area to the north of the main terminal complex is being developed for industrial use. All this work has had a positive impact, with Vienna awarded a four-star rating by Skytrax.

There has been an airfield at Schwechat since 1938
Flughafen Wien

Concourse D, also known as Pier East, is used for non-Schengen destinations, housing gates D21 to D29 (airbridges), D31 to D36 (buses) and D61 to D70 (buses)
Key-Robert Veitch

Austrian Airlines A320neo, OE-LZP (c/n 11418), has been with the airline since June 2023 and is one of five neos in the fleet
Austrian Airlines

Bonjour
Ajaccio

> The broad, soft, sandy beaches offer expansive panoramic views, towards the city on one side and the end of the runway on the other — catering to the aviation geek and sun worshipper in equal measure

For those in search of a short escape offering beaches, culture, panoramas and aviation, follow the footsteps of **Robert Veitch** on a flying visit to the capital of Corsica

There has been an airfield at Ajaccio since 1935 *Alamy/ Camille Moirenc – Hemis.fr*

Ajaccio Napoleon Bonaparte Airport is the primary aerial gateway into the island of Corsica, linking the adjacent capital city of Ajaccio with mainland France. The airport is named after Napoleon Bonaparte, he of the Battle of Waterloo and later exile in Saint Helena, who was born in Ajaccio in 1769. His birthplace and ancestral home, Maison Bonaparte, is now a museum.

A grass airfield formed the first runway in 1935 when it was known as Campo dell'Oro – the field of gold – located on the fertile alluvial plain of the Gravona and Prunelli rivers. A new east-west runway 10/28 was created at the start of World War Two, but the unpaved surface lacked the strength to welcome all but the smallest of aircraft. On September 9, 1943, the people of Ajaccio rose up against the occupying Nazi forces to become the first liberated city in France, and the act is commemorated on a plaque on a marble plinth beneath three flagpoles, alongside the drop-off zone. The following year, the US Air Force laid down metal grids to make 10/28 a hard runway, and in the months that followed a temporary terminal and new hard north-south runway was constructed to form the basis of the modern facility. In time, 10/28 would become disused, though its remains are clearly visible.

A new terminal and air traffic control tower opened in 1961 when the airport was welcoming Douglas DC-3s and DC-4s. Air France introduced the first jets in the 1960s, flying Sud Aviation SE-210 Caravelles from Paris, Marseille and Nice. Package tours began arriving a decade later, bringing tourism to the region, fulfilling the needs of sun-seekers, and boosting the local economy. Charter carriers such as Air Liberté, Corse Air, Minerve, Euralair, Europe Aero Service and Touraine Air Transport, plus Dan Air and Britannia Airways from the UK were all regular visitors. For a period in the 1990s, Air France flew Boeing 747-200s and then -400s into Ajaccio from Paris/Orly during peak periods at the weekend. Although it can handle widebodies, the relatively short runway and the horseshoe of higher ground and mountains have always made the airport a challenge for larger jets.

As the millennium turned, it processed more than one million

The climate is positively Mediterranean, offering temperatures of 20°C for more than half the year and the vibe is maritime, with flotillas of boats and yachts in the harbour. Cruise ships are also prevalent in the harbour, though connections are sluggish in comparison with air travel, with Nice taking up to eight hours, Porto Torres four, Toulon ten and Marseille 13. The harbour side is reminiscent of the Cote d'Azur, offering pastel shades, terracotta tiles and tree-lined boulevards – café culture, tranquil and walkable, with extensive views into the Golfe d'Ajaccio and the distant aircraft using the airport.

Napoleon's gateway

Located four miles and 15-20 minutes from the city centre, the facility is close to the action, yet far enough away to be on the periphery. During 2023, it processed 37% of the air traffic to and from the island, ahead of other Corsican airports at Bastia, Calvi and Figari. Around 80% of all flights operated are to or from Marseille, Nice and Paris/Orly, with Lyon and Toulouse being the other year-round routes.

It's the primary hub of flag carrier, Air Corsica, which operates a fleet of ATR 72-600s and Airbus A320s, and has its MRO hangar and corporate offices located on the eastern fringe of the airfield. It operates Public Service

Arrive in the spring and visitors are likely to see snow atop the distant summits that form the spine of the mountainous island
All images Key-Robert Veitch unless stated

Baggage collection carousels in the arrivals hall

passengers in a year for the first time. With passenger numbers increasing, a new, more spacious terminal was opened in 2004 and remains in use to the present day. During 2012, the facility processed 1,218,705 passengers. By the end of 2024 that number had climbed to 1,605,212 and aircraft movements totalled 14,024 to place it among the top 15 busiest airports in France.

Touching down

Final approach is either across the Golfe d'Ajaccio or between the mountains, but once on the ground aircraft park diagonally to the terminal. With an absence of airbridges, terra firma is accessed via airstairs and lungfuls of coastal air. The stroll to arrivals passes the departures frontage with its banked lawns, manicured shrubbery and palm trees, offering a unique and genial je ne sais quoi. Arrive in the spring and visitors are likely to see snow atop the distant summits that form the spine of the mountainous island. Half a dozen steps up lead into arrivals proper, at the northern end of the building, where there are a couple of baggage carousels and passport control. Landside there is car hire, buses and taxis, plus car parking offering 1,500 spaces, covering kiss and fly, short and long-stay.

Ajaccio

Corsica is approximately 110 miles southeast of Nice, 55 miles west of Tuscany, seven miles north of Sardinia, and has been a part of France since 1780. Ajaccio is on the west of the island, at the base and lower slopes of wooded hills on the northern side of the bay. It is the largest settlement on Corsica – the population of 75,000 making up a significant chunk of the island's 355,500 souls. The citadel at the entrance to the harbour guards the entrance to the city and its narrow streets.

From the terminal it's approximately 400m to the nearest beach – catering to the aviation geek and sun worshipper in equal measure

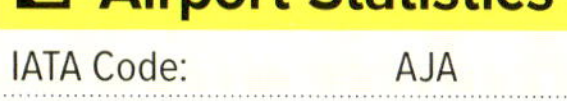

Obligation (PSO) routes to Nice and Marseille and shares the Paris/Orly PSO route with Air France, which usually operates A320 Family aircraft on its flights. Both airlines operate year-round, and their services are augmented by seasonal operations from Amelia International, Chalair Aviation, easyJet, Luxair, Norwegian Air Shuttle, Transavia and Volotea. The airport currently facilitates 28 routes of which five are permanent. Seasonal services operate to five countries, incorporating rotations to Charleroi, Geneva, Luxembourg, Oslo/Gardermoen, Rome/Fiumicino, Venice/Marco Polo and Zurich. With a significant number of summer seasonal services, Saturday is usually the busiest day for movements.

There are various spotters' sites around the airfield perimeter where aircraft movements can be viewed and photographed. But... from the terminal it's approximately 400m of level walking to the broad, soft, sandy beaches and expansive panoramic views, towards the city on one side and the end of the runway on the other – catering to the aviation geek and sun worshipper in equal measure.

Triste au revoir

Approached from Route de Campo dell'Oro, the tarmac is lined with sand on either side and the sea to the right. As the airport nears, elderly windswept pine trees populate either side of the road, almost an arboreal guard of honour wishing departing passengers a safe onward journey. On final approach, the shallow curved roof sections that span the terminal are clear to see, offering a subtle nod towards aircraft wings and flaps. The current terminal is approximately 130m in length, covers 180,000sq ft, and has capacity for 1.5 million passengers per year.

Inside, departures operate from the opposing end of the ground floor to arrivals. Plenty of natural light spills down from the vaulted ceiling, reducing the requirement for electrical light during daylight hours. There's a café with seating for around 50 people offering views of the apron, a dozen check-in desks, some self-check-in consoles, an information desk and a small shop. Security is compact, but for much of the year it is all the facility requires, as flights per day hover around ten – but those busy summer Saturdays might be a different story.

The departure lounge feels a little compressed in comparison to the main concourse, but it serves its purpose, housing five gates lettered A to E, and offers wonderful floor-to-ceiling views of the apron and mountains beyond. A duty free shop is well stocked with local delicacies and regional delights. When the flight is called it's a sad goodbye, departing being the reverse of arrival excitement; down six steps, before strolling to the aircraft, inhaling the last of the Corsican air. A final look back, a hankering for more, the end of a flying visit. ✈

Approaching the airport, pine trees on either side of the road seemingly form a guard of honour wishing departing passengers a safe onward journey

Plenty of natural light spills down through the vaulted ceiling in the check-in area

There are worse views to be had from a departure lounge!

The **psychology** of the **airport**

Dr Nicola Davies unravels the complex subject of passenger psychology within the airport environment and examines what can be done to improve the traveller experience

Jewel at Singapore/Changi contains the world's tallest indoor waterfall, and receives around 300,000 visitors daily
Changi Airport Group

n July 2014, Singapore's Changi Airport announced its intention to continue its efforts to improve the travelling experience: "We want to offer a stress-free and smooth experience to those going through Changi," Teng Lye Teck, executive vice president of Changi Airport Group, told BBC reporter Puneet Pal Singh. In particular, Terminal 4, then under construction, was designed to incorporate automated self-check-in facilities, offering passengers the ability to tag and drop their bags themselves. The aim was to cut waiting times, but more importantly the adaptation showed a growing awareness that the airport has a lot to gain from travellers who are in a happier, less stressed mood. For a start, shorter queuing times mean travellers will have more time to spend in retail outlets and be in less need of assistance from airport employees.

So, what is it about the airport experience that is so stressful and how can airport

employees take a leaf out of Changi's book to ensure travelling is an altogether more pleasant experience – for everyone?

Fight or flight – literally

Research has shown that airports are among the most stressful places to visit, with 25% of people in the UK rating airports as equally as worrying as moving house. The stress response is a natural physiological mechanism designed to alert us to potential threats in the environment, creating the fight or flight response. While this was important in evolutionary terms for survival, our physiology hasn't caught up with the changing world. Therefore, anything different to our usual, everyday experience, can trigger the fight or flight response – including busy airports.

The causes of airport stress are obvious and endless – queues, crowds, enhanced security checkpoints, delays, and baggage checks. For some, just finding the correct gate and being on time can be an exhausting challenge. Some research indicates that up to one in ten of us avoid flying altogether because it is considered too stressful.

Here are some of the reasons attributed to the stress experienced by so many travellers:

Lack of control – When people believe they are in control of a situation they can manage stressful events far more effectively. In the same way, when people pass through airports, feeling unsure about what might happen next is a common experience. This sense of being out of control is what leads to increased stress. Indeed, survey data suggests that the most stressful parts of the airport experience relate to feelings of 'lack of control' – flight delays, losing luggage, and getting to the gate on time all rely on factors often outside the individual's control.

Crowds – Many studies have demonstrated links with crowded environments and stress. Busy environments can be unpredictable and produce a feeling of 'sensory overload', there is just too much information for the brain to process. Airports deal with a high density of people; combine this with delays, queues, and unfamiliar surroundings and you've got a highly stressful experience. London/Heathrow is one of the world's busiest international airports, with more than 80 million passengers passing through it in 2024. It is not surprising, therefore, that Heathrow was cited in one survey as being the most stressful airport in the UK.

Deadlines – While time deadlines are not unique to airports, combined

Singapore/Changi's Terminal 4 was designed to provide passengers with a relaxing and efficient place from which to fly
Changi Airport Group

> " The causes of airport stress are obvious and endless – queues, crowds, enhanced security checkpoints, delays, and baggage checks "

Above: **Queuing is a stressful pet hate for almost every passenger, but airports are doing much to tackle this issue with online and mobile check-in, bag-drops and larger security screening areas** *Key-Mark Nicholls*

Right: **The security screening process is one of the most stressful parts of the flying experience, particularly for infrequent flyers who may not be familiar with current requirements** *Gatwick Airport/Justin Lambert*

with the other stressful aspects within the terminals, time urgency frequently becomes amplified. One survey showed that 37% of respondents report anxiety due to worries about running late. An interesting behavioural way of measuring time urgency is through walking speed – passengers will often increase their pace because of fear of being late or being unsure of where to go. As with any busy environment they may just get 'swept along' with the fast average rate. In 2007, The University of Hertfordshire's professor Richard Wiseman said: "When you speed up, [people] become stressed." In other words, feeling the need to walk quickly or being 'swept along' can contribute to increased stress.

Accumulation effects – Stressors have a habit of accumulating, with new ones appearing before previous ones have been resolved. For example, if a person is anxious the night before travelling, this anxiety can be exacerbated if they experience stress at the airport the following day. If people are in a stressed state already, hassles at airports can have a compound effect. Research indicates people may be stressed before they even set foot in the terminal. In a CPP survey, 13% said getting lost on the way to the airport made them stressed and 14% were put at a heightened level of anxiety by finding somewhere to park.

Three traveller types

A key psychological factor involved in airport stress is perception – how we process the experience. A look at the psychology of the airport suggests there are three types of traveller employees can look out for – the worriers, warriors and adventurers. For worriers, the lack of control they experience can cause high levels of distress. These same

conditions can be a source of excitement for adventurers, who enjoy the whole air travel experience. For seasoned travellers, also known as warriors, airport stressors are just accepted. They travel frequently, often on business, and can normally be spotted by their calm, resigned demeanour.

Handling these three disparate groups are the airport employees. For the average worker, a traveller's experience doesn't appear to be something that can be improved upon. After all, employees can do little to change queue length and security check protocols. Fortunately, however, it is possible to change the travellers' perceptions regarding these inevitabilities. Despite the warrior and adventurer already having a mindset that assists them through the airport experience, small courtesies can go a long way with these two types of traveller. Making a customer feel important costs little and any successful restaurant owner will attest to the importance of building rapport with their most valuable customers.

For airport employees, the most demanding customers will be the worriers, but fortunately, nervous energy and anxiety are malleable. The crucial thing is to isolate what is causing the anxiety, address it and find a more pleasurable focus for the worrier's attention.

Queues – Workers can assist passengers by making sure they have correct documentation and are in the right queue. If travellers are legitimately running late, depending on airport and airline regulations, it might be possible

to expedite them through the queues, so they don't miss their flight. If it's simply that people are expressing aggravation at having to wait, it is worth trying to engage their sense of adventure by asking them about their destination. If they're thinking about what they'll do when they arrive, the time in the queue will pass more quickly.

Security – This can be particularly frightening for the worrier so they should be made aware of what will be expected when it is their turn. Metal items in the provided trays, boarding pass in hand, and any other requirements that are necessary. It may also be necessary to assure passengers of the speed and professionalism of security. Workers need to be prepared to answer questions about body scans and pat-downs. Often a fear of the unknown is far worse than anything that will actually happen.

Navigation – For worriers this part can be more stressful than the queues and information is the best way to combat anxiety in this situation. Not only can workers help lost passengers find their gates, but they can also take a moment to explain the layout of the terminal and any coding used on the gate number. Explaining the easiest way to the gate or where refreshments can be found can also be reassuring. At international airports, assistance can be as simple as guiding travellers in the direction of luggage collection, a helpdesk, or an exit point.

For worriers the flight can be a terrifying experience, but staff can help foster a feeling of passenger safety which will create positive attitudes, which in turn will minimise the stress experienced by everyone *Air Astana*

Another common fear among travellers is that of losing their luggage
American Airlines

In-flight – For the true worrier, the flight itself can be an entirely terrifying experience, and it's important that any concerns are treated seriously. Workers should not give the danger itself merit – only the question. Fostering a feeling of safety in passengers will create positive attitudes, which in turn will minimise the stress experienced by everyone. Instead of just saying that everything is fine, staff should take a few extra moments and explain why they know everything is fine.

Biophilic design

It might seem like the responsibility of ensuring a less stressful experience is all down to airport employees. However, this is far from the case and research has shown that terminal architecture also plays a role in the travel experience. Curved surfaces, warm lighting, and greenery in passenger areas have been found to have a calming and reassuring effect. This is due to such designs being associated with nature.

We all have an inbuilt affinity to nature – also known as biophilia. One study showed that 95% of all individuals in a stressful situation felt that being outdoors was the most effective way ↘

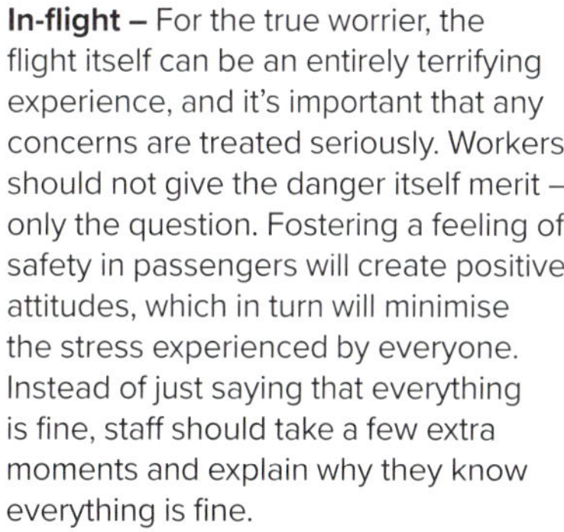

Clear and simple signage, like at Helsinki, is vitally important in keeping passengers calm and allowing them to navigate a terminal
Key-Robert Veitch

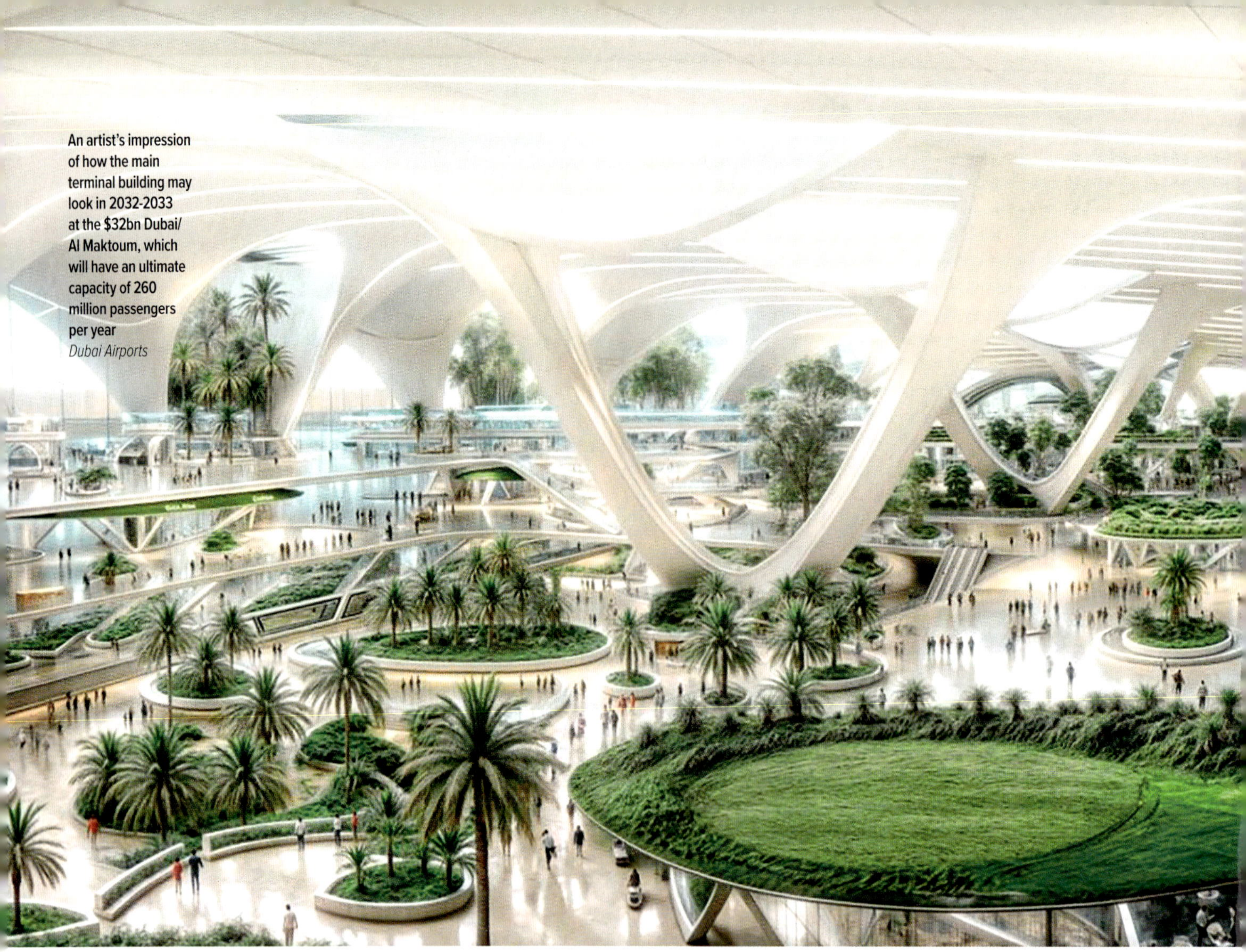

An artist's impression of how the main terminal building may look in 2032-2033 at the $32bn Dubai/Al Maktoum, which will have an ultimate capacity of 260 million passengers per year *Dubai Airports*

to alleviate stress. Architects are making the most of this by utilising space, lighting, aesthetics, and the outside world in airport architecture; basically, bringing nature indoors. A better understanding of biophilia has led to an increase in the use of biomimicry, which imitates the basic principles of nature in order to inspire innovative architecture – including in terminals. In particular, bringing greenery indoors has been used effectively to reduce passenger agitation, and views of the natural landscape are also very well received.

Even the soothing sounds of a fountain or music can reduce anxiety. Detroit/Metropolitan Wayne County in Michigan, offers an excellent example having installed 9,000ft of glass panelling incorporating LED displays set to music into the 700ft long terminal connecting Concourse A with Concourse B/C – which has become an airside attraction in its own right.

Art is another method of bringing some of the outdoors into passenger areas; colour also plays a role in generating an emotional response.

For some, just finding the correct gate and being on time can be an exhausting challenge and this sense of being out of control is what leads to increased stress *Frankfurt Airport*

In particular, boarding gates and waiting areas in warm earthy tones or soft ocean hues are effective for lowering stress levels and evoking a positive mood. Seeing colour sets off a reaction within the brain, which in turn activates the autonomic nervous system – the control centre for our heart rate and blood pressure.

Red, for example, stimulates the adrenal gland responsible for releasing the hormones that respond to stress. Seeing red causes heart rate and blood pressure to increase and, in so doing, increases alertness and vitality. At the other end of the spectrum, blue has the effect of lowering blood pressure and heart rate. Yellow, on the other hand, has a completely different influence on the mind and body, affecting the thyroid gland. This part of our hormonal system controls how quickly the body uses its available energy by stimulating the brain and nerves which, in turn, makes the muscles feel more energetic. Pictures showing blue seas or yellow sunny days could greatly improve the airport experience.

Colour is essentially a refraction of certain wavelengths found in the natural light spectrum. Therefore, it makes sense that the use of phototherapy to harness the beneficial effects of light can be similarly used in airport settings to reduce anxiety. Using as much natural lighting as possible in airport

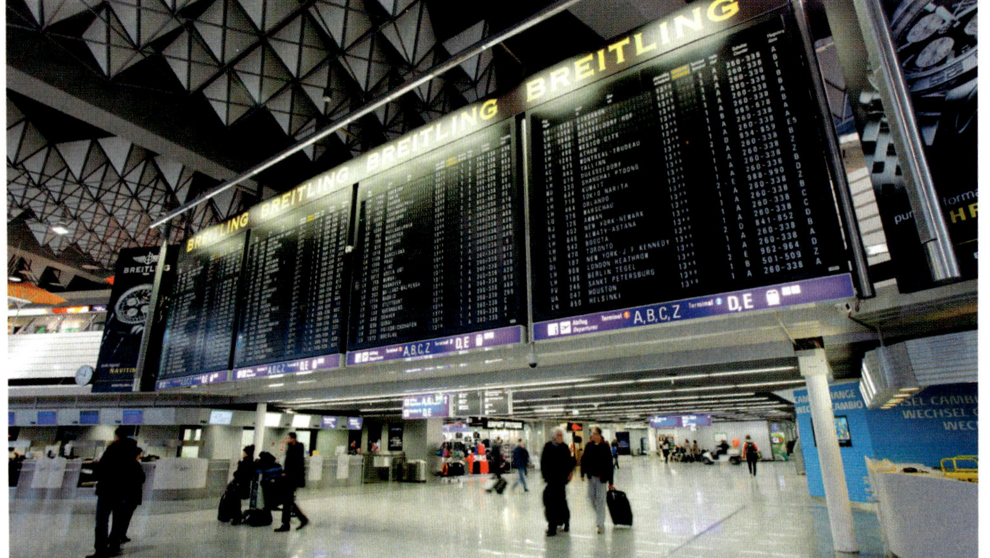

public areas, for example, could help to increase serotonin levels, which are essential for positive feelings. Full spectrum or natural light is also essential for reducing our response to stress hormones such as the adrenocorticotropic hormone (ACTH).

These hormones are responsible for our fight-or-flight response in dangerous situations which can build up in response to stress, including the anxiety experienced in the terminal.

Dallas/Fort Worth and Charlotte/Douglas have both incorporated these concepts into their security checkpoints. Wall coverings have pastel-coloured mood lighting and pictures of natural scenes such as flowers and water cascades intended for calming frayed nerves. The trays for personal belongings have been similarly decorated with different shades of green and blue. Even the furniture has been changed from impersonal metal and plastic to warmer, natural tones of wood and leather.

And relax...

In 2014, Shashank Nigam, CEO of aviation marketing consultancy SimpliFlying said: "Travellers are looking for something more than just a transactional experience, they want something more emotional." As such, Singapore/Changi has introduced more technology to entice passengers including a mini-cinema, swimming pool, free massage chairs and even a butterfly garden. Thanks to these improvements, a clear focus on the traveller experience, and continued evolution of the airport terminal, not just in Singapore, but around the world, means that the moving forwards the passenger experience should continue to improve year on year. ✈

Natural building materials and plenty of light help make the check-in at Madrid/Barajas Terminal 4 a calm experience *Madrid Airport*

The light tunnel connecting the two piers of the McNamara Terminal at Detroit/Metropolitan has become an attraction in its own right *Detroit Metropolitan Airport*

Double

Richard Schuurman speaks with key figures to learn why Amsterdam's Schiphol Airport is the subject of fierce political debate about aircraft movement caps as it plans for future growth

Dutch

Say 'Amsterdam Schiphol' to seasoned travellers, and you'll likely get a positive response from most. Many rate the Dutch airport highly for its connectivity (there were 301 available destinations last year), on-time performance and one-terminal concept – although walking distances can be extended. That's been the perception for decades, with the hub constantly investing to prepare for ever-growing passenger numbers.

But growth has a downside and there is growing opposition in the wider Amsterdam area against noise pollution, emissions and the impact on healthcare. Schiphol has been the topic of heated political debate in the Dutch parliament that is continuing. The Dutch government intends to cap annual capacity to 478,000 movements this November, the outcome of a 'Balanced Approach' procedure, but this has been met with strong opposition from the aviation sector.

A panoramic view over D-pier, most of Schiphol airport and Amsterdam in the distance *Schiphol Airport/P Bakker*

KLM Royal Dutch Airlines is inseparably related to Schiphol, operating aircraft of all sizes and accounting for 250,000 of the 473,815 aircraft movements during 2024 *Vincenzo Pace*

Connected

Schiphol began life as a tiny military airfield on September 19, 1916, and became a civil airfield in 1920 when KLM launched commercial services. It was completely destroyed in World War Two then rebuilt on the original site, before opening a new terminal on its current footprint in 1967, immediately becoming one of the most modern airports in the world, hailed for its 'all under one roof' concept.

The airport and flag carrier are inseparably related, each benefiting from the other. For the airline, the airport is instrumental to its hub-and-spoke network that has made the gateway popular with transit passengers. From 105,500 movements in 1970, numbers doubled to 202,300 in 1990, and 414,900 in 2000. After a decade of ups and downs, there were 386,300 movements and 45.1 million passengers in 2010.

Since then, the numbers have mostly grown and, by 2015, they stood at 451,000 movements and 58.2 million passengers, peaking at 499,444 movements in 2018, and 71.7 million passengers in 2019. That dropped to 52.5 million in 2022, a year remembered for utter chaos as understaffing at security and ground handling resulted in queues that extended outside the terminal buildings as Schiphol's reputation fell below subzero. By the end of last year the hub had bounced back, processing 66.8 million passengers and 473,815 movements.

Ongoing debate

During COVID-19, residents in the crowded city of Amsterdam and the municipality of Haarlemmermeer got used to better sleep and quieter days, only to be confronted with post-pandemic reality as air travel recovered.

Lounge 1 dates back to 1967, but will offer an additional 5,000m² of lighter and brighter passenger space from July 2025 *Schiphol Airport*

It reignited a social and political debate about the size of Schiphol that goes back to 2008, when the government embraced a noise reduction plan to transfer 70,000 flights to Eindhoven Airport and the to-be-developed Lelystad Airport 40 miles northeast of Schiphol.

Over the past 17 years, the debate has become fiercer and increasingly complex. A couple of years ago it became apparent that Schiphol had been operating without a valid nature permit for years – its existing Luchthavenbesluit (airport operating permit) is outdated, and noise levels were exceeding regulatory levels. Multiple high court rulings since 2019 on excessive nitrogen oxide emissions have affected the planning process across the Netherlands and also affect aviation. The public debate about Schiphol has become extremely sensitive and tense, notably on social media, yet

despite the opposition to flying, nine million Dutch citizens (half the population) used the airport last year.

In June 2022, Mark Harbers, then minister of transportation and water management, announced a two-step experimental rule to cap capacity at Schiphol. The first step was to reduce movements from 500,000 to around 452,500 by late 2023, then a second reduction to 440,000 from late 2024 after a 'Balanced Approach' procedure. The experimental rule resulted in a court case from airlines and IATA, which they initially won but subsequently lost in the appeal court. Harbers withdrew the experimental rule after the US Department of Transportation and the European Commission (EC) threatened retaliatory measures, believing the cap contravened bilateral agreements.

The reduction plan to 440,000 movements was delayed then modified

EasyJet is the second-biggest operator at Schiphol and is based at H-pier *Richard Schuurman*

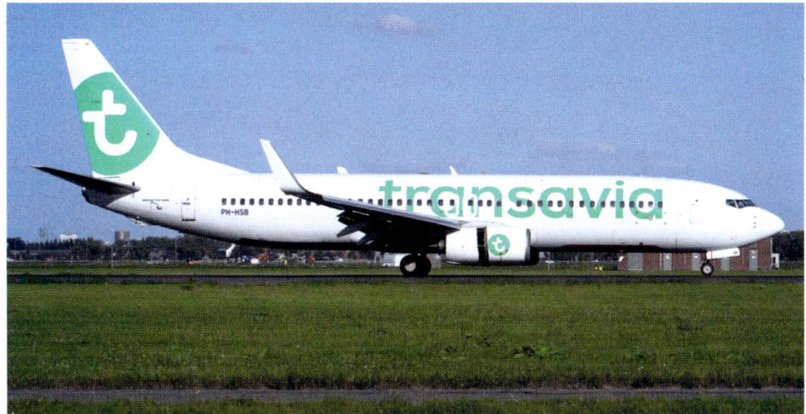

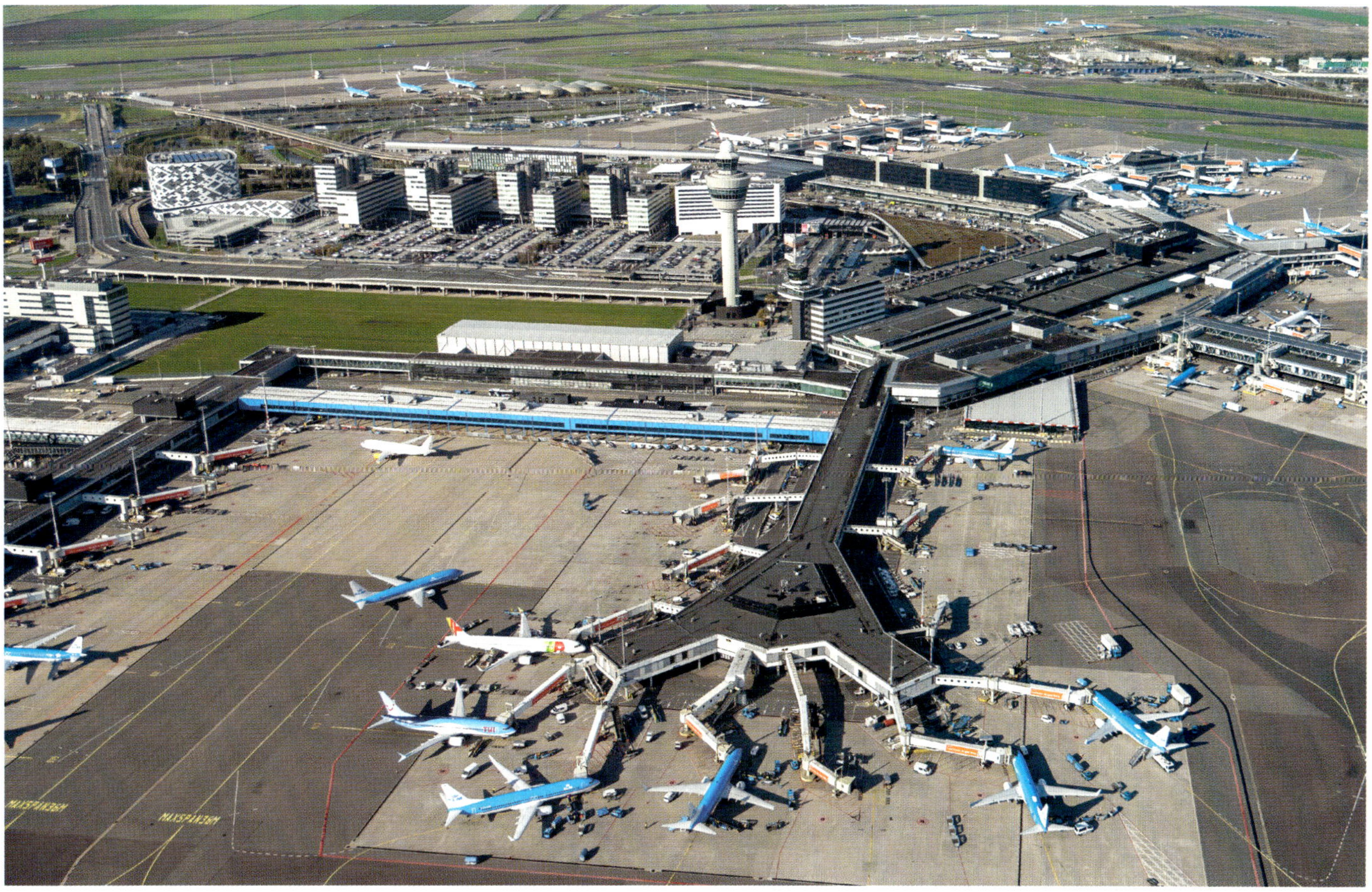

under minister Barry Madlener, who took office in 2024. His aim has been to end polarisation between the opposing camps, but he caused a stir during an interview when he said that people who couldn't stand an airport as their neighbour should move. Madlener also opposes plans for 80,000 houses in the Schiphol area, resulting in accusations from opposing parliamentary parties, that he is too cosy with the aviation sector.

In the latest version of the 'Balanced Approach', Madlener intends to cap capacity to 478,000 movements this November. The number in itself isn't a final target but a means to reduce noise and pollution levels – initially it's a 15% reduction instead of the original 20% target. The package requires KLM and its subsidiary Transavia to operate quieter aircraft during the night, additional fleet renewal from all airlines, a reduction of flights between 11pm and 7am from 32,000 to 27,000 annually, plus higher fees for noisy aircraft. A reduction of 5,000 historical slots is inevitable, although Madlener expects they can be found without many problems. Once this package has been monitored, a follow-on package might be introduced for the remaining 5% of noise reduction.

During April in the Dutch parliament, Madlener said: "Under the current permit, 500,000 movements are allowed, 440,000 didn't make me and the sector happy, but a reduction to 478,000 is a huge reduction in movements and hindrances. It isn't causing too much pain to airlines but will hurt them. It still can't be ruled out that US carriers will retaliate. It's the first time that KLM will not be able to grow unconditionally, but this package safeguards the future of Schiphol and improves livability for citizens around the airport."

Even before the cap is applied in November, Schiphol has implemented its own measures to stimulate the use of quieter aircraft by introducing higher fees in April, as Robert Carsouw, the company's chief financial officer explained during a parliamentary session: "Night flights will be six times more expensive than day flights. Notably, the use of Boeing 747 freighters will be charged heavily. Whereas we charge €900 for an A350 during the day, a 747-400F will go to €16,000 during night hours. One of our biggest foreign airlines is committed to ↘

Above: **C-pier, seen here in 2021, is the oldest pier at the Dutch gateway and will be completely demolished and replaced from 2027** *Schiphol Airport/ P Bakker*

Left: **A cap on night flights might hurt Transavia, which operates 40 Boeing 737-800s including PH-HSB (c/n 34172)** *Vincenzo Pace*

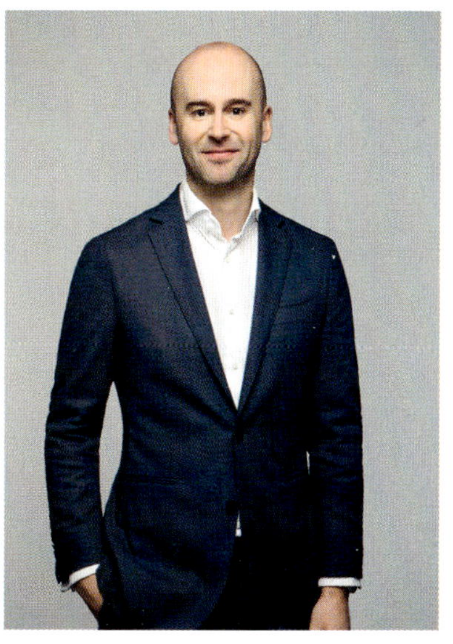

Sybren Hahn is chief infrastructure officer of the Royal Schiphol Group *Schiphol Airport/P Bakker*

Above: C-pier is more or less unchanged since it was erected in 1967 and at 18m wide is deemed too narrow for modern use *Richard Schuurman*

Above middle: Construction work continues on the €1.4bn four-storey A-pier, seen here in 2023, which has been subject to a legal dispute between the airport and the construction firms *Schiphol Airport/ J Berends*

Below: An artist's impression of the new 13-gate modular C-pier, where construction will begin in 2027 once A-pier is operational *Schiphol Airport/ Space&Matter*

> ## The airport and flag carrier are inseparably related, each benefitting from the other

growing the share of its quietest aircraft this summer from 35% to 60%. Thanks to commitments like these, we expect to meet the targeted 15% reduction in noise this November by and large, and possibly even 17%."

KLM

A reduction will hurt KLM by 4,600 movements a year at a cost of half a million passengers. Of 473,815 movements at Schiphol last year, KLM used 250,000 and its leisure subsidiary Transavia took 32,000. EasyJet is the second-biggest operator with 34,000 movements.

Marjan Rintel, president/CEO of KLM, is concerned and said in parliament: "It's not just about the economic interests of KLM, but about our welfare. Everywhere in Europe, airports can grow, look at Copenhagen, Madrid or the recent plans of London Heathrow. Thanks to our carefully developed network, we can explore the world and are the home of many renowned companies. Reducing capacity and taxing air travel simply results in traffic, businesses and jobs going abroad. It doesn't benefit [the] climate when holiday travellers will opt to fly from Belgium or Germany."

Both Rintel and Marcel de Nooijer, Transavia CEO, have said the night cap specifically affects the low-cost carrier. Rintel said: "The night is very important to us, not just for cargo but also for Transavia. Many leisure flights depart during the night. They have already inducted many Airbus A321neos, but are now penalised without being offered an alternative." Her view has also been addressed by the EC when it examined the 'Balanced Approach' package in March. Both highlighted the government only partly includes the effects of fleet renewal and excludes various operational measures that help to reduce noise. "We invest €7bn euros in new aircraft," said Rintel. "But I can't explain to others why only 15 out of 61 are included in calculations for noise reduction. The Department of Transportation says the other aircraft are autonomous growth, but these 46 [also] have a significant positive impact on noise solution." Excluding those is "unacceptable," she pointed out.

Madlener is of the view that he has correctly followed the 'Balanced Approach'. However, in April, airlines including KLM, TUI fly and easyJet, plus IATA and stakeholder organisations sought another court ruling but were declared inadmissible. They were advised to present their case to the Raad van State (Council of State), which has both an advisory and judicial role. At the end of April, the council in its advisory role stated that the minister should better substantiate his capacity reduction, sidelining with EC Commissioner Apostolos Tzitzikostas who also asked for clarification. Yet, on May 7, Madlener notified parliament that he would pursue his capacity and interim operating plan in November without further changes.

Investment time

Meanwhile, Schiphol is preparing for the future and, in a diversion from recent history, it increased year-on-year charges by an average of 41.4% this April, with another 7.6% due next year and 12.5% in 2027. It caused major outrage among airlines, but the airport says the incremental revenues are essential for its €6bn, five-year investment plan announced last August, partly allocated for refurbishment of existing infrastructure. When he entered office in June 2024, Pieter van Oord, the new CEO of Royal Schiphol Group, was appalled by the state of some basic facilities, with buckets standing under leaking roofs, outdated washrooms, or inoperable moving walkways that immediately impacted the passenger experience. Other facilities for airport crew are also poor and inadequate, so Van Oord made it a top priority to sort this out, and now more than 400 projects are in preparation or progress, to transform Schiphol.

Sybren Hahn, chief infrastructure officer, is overseeing these projects. He admitted the focus had been on growth and cost reductions for too many years since 2010, to make Schiphol the cheapest of the major European airports: "Constant outsourcing did result in a race to the bottom for staffing, culminating in the shortages and issues we faced in 2022.

"Less visible was that our assets suffered from a lack of investment. We calculated that we underinvested some half a billion euros in our basic infrastructure and delayed key projects, like the refurbishment of C-pier. Since 2005, passenger numbers have grown by 27 million without any growth in terminal and apron facilities. There's overdue maintenance and we are significantly short on capacity. By passengers per square metre, we are one of the busiest airports in Europe."

Lounges 1 and 2

This July, the refurbishment of Lounge 1 for Schengen passengers into a larger and lighter space will be completed, as Hahn explained: "Lounge 1 is the oldest terminal that dates back to 1967. All technical infrastructure needed replacement. We created 5,000m² of additional passenger space by sacrificing offices. We eliminated bottlenecks by separating passenger flows using the new square metres, bringing in more light and adding a seating area that overlooks the apron."

The offering of shops and restaurants has been improved, as Hahn noted: "There are more of both of them, with a range of concepts for our passengers to improve their experience at the airport. In the centre of Lounge 1 there is a shopping island, which is an example of our new shopping experience and also helps to split traffic movements, as people can pass by from two sides. In the past, it was really tight sometimes near the transfer desk area and the Bubbles Bar, [but] the rearrangement and new wayfinding should improve passenger flows."

Lounge 2 is a few years younger, so extensive updates are not required so soon, but there will be some upgrades, as Hahn explained: "Shopping wise, Lounge 2 will see another step in

Above: Lounge 2 is a few years younger than Lounge 1, so extensive updates are not currently required *Schiphol Airport/R Cremers*

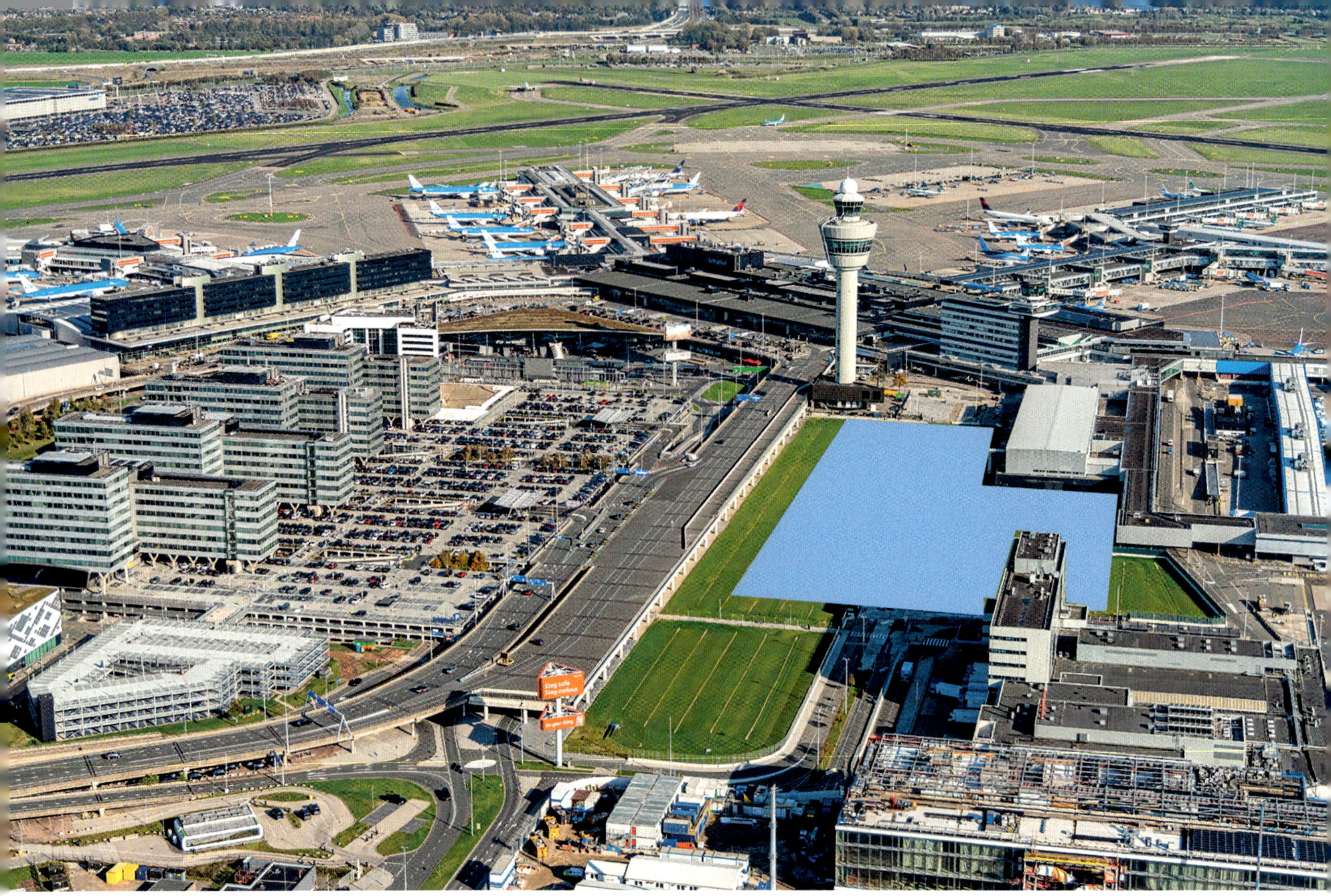

Construction on the new 20,000m^2 baggage basement will begin in 2026, with completion set for 2031 at the earliest. The site could also be the location of a new terminal *Schiphol Airport*

becoming a luxury world – Louis Vuitton will open one of its biggest shops. Longer term, we foresee growing capacity issues in both Lounge 1 and 2 as airlines upgauge their fleets and operate bigger aircraft, like the Airbus A321neo.

This translates [as] 20% more passengers per aircraft that will be felt on peak hours."

A and C-piers

Renewal of C-pier has been postponed for years but is scheduled for mid-2027. Essentially, it is unchanged from 1967, except for an additional nine gates built in 1971. Hahn said: "C-pier will be completely demolished and replaced by a new one in a modular build concept. The current one is 18m wide, but modern piers are 35-40m, [and] through that we get additional space at the gates to accommodate larger aircraft and more passengers." The new version will retain 13 gates, and be accessible to larger aircraft, but the current characteristic multi-gate furthest end will disappear for practical reasons, as he explained: "In the current layout, aircraft are pushed back onto taxiway alpha, which causes traffic jams and safety issues. At the new pier, we push back sideways onto the apron."

The renewal of the C-pier will only start once the new A-pier is operational in mid-2027. The four-storey building that looks like a dedicated concourse was supposed to open in 2019, but the airport and its two construction companies got into a dispute that went to court in April. The builders accused Schiphol of failing to provide the correct drawings and specifications, and the airport claimed build quality was below standard and required remedial work. A-pier is now being completed, but the budget has more than doubled to €1.4bn.

Hahn said: "Construction should be complete in December 2026. We will start our operational readiness tests and acceptance tests after that for opening in mid-2027. A-pier is multifunctional [and] initially, it will operate as a Schengen area, especially when we are reconstructing C-pier. But we have two floors for screened and non-screened non-Schengen passengers." A-pier will have 11 gates for narrowbodies or six for widebodies when used at the same time. Even after its completion, the A-pier B-pier platform for KLM Cityhopper and other regional carriers will remain in use.

On what is currently unused land between A and C-piers, a new baggage basement will begin construction in 2026, with completion set for 2031 at the earliest. It will offer 20,000m^2 of additional capacity, but Hahn noted: "We also need it as we plan to refurbish the existing cellar under D-pier, which is used for 40% of all luggage capacity and most of the transfer flights. Systems are very old there – we are one of only two airports in the world that still uses the handling system, [and] we even buy spare parts from other airports to keep it running." Future plans include the refurbishment of the luggage basement under E-pier.

New terminal

Even with pier upgrades and a new baggage basement, Schiphol is never complete and non-Schengen Lounge 3 and low-cost Lounge 4 might see

Schiphol's panoramic terrace offers extensive views of the airfield, plus access to retired KLM Fokker 70, PH-OFE (c/n11260), which last flew in 2003 *Richard Schuurman*

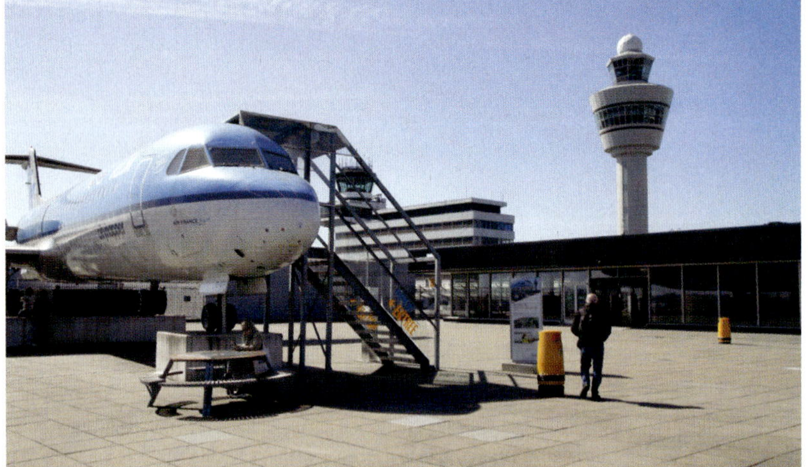

KLM Airbus A321neo, PH-AXA (c/n 11895), was the first of the type to join the fleet in August 2024
Richard Schuurman

concept. The second is Location Northwest, between Motorways A4 and A9 and adjacent to runway 36C/18C, but the remote location would require extensive connectivity to the current terminals plus new road and rail infrastructure. Hahn remained tight-lipped about a preference: "Some considerations are how this location would solve our capacity constraints, what the impact is on our neighbours, and how passengers and our staff will experience it. It's a big puzzle we want to complete this year."

Uncertainty continues. In June, the government (and Madlener) resigned while a court revoked the 2023 nature permit. Yet, Schiphol still targets a return to the top three European airports.

upgrades and extensions. Airport management is evaluating where to build another terminal, with a decision due this year, as Hahn explained: "Even when our capacity will remain at 478,000 movements for years to come, we still need another terminal. Currently, we accommodate a large fleet of smaller, regional aircraft thanks to KLM Cityhopper, but as aircraft grow bigger, we require more space per passenger. In 2035, we forecast 25% more passengers and will likely process over 80 million passengers in 2030. A new terminal is not about growth, it's about facilitating capacity."

There are two options: one is Location South on top of the new luggage basement, which is the most obvious as it maintains Schiphol's one-terminal

Left: **KLM President and CEO Marjan Rintel meets Barry Madlener, Dutch Minister of Transportation and Water Management**
Richard Schuurman

Below: **Looking over G-Pier, F-Pier and E-Pier to D-Pier in the distance**
Schiphol Airport

> " Airport management is evaluating where to build another terminal, with a decision due this year "

A Pan American World Airways Airbus A310-200 roars out of Berlin/Tegel in February 1988. The airline later ceased operations on December 4, 1991, and the airport waved off its final flight on November 8, 2020 *Ullstein Bild/ Getty Images*

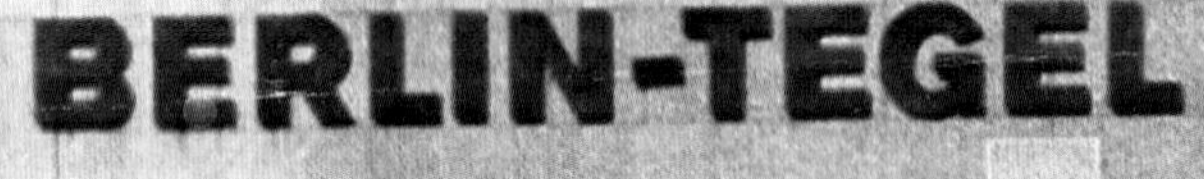

PAN AM
AEG
BABCOCK
BORSIG

Final call for Gate 101

There are times in the line of duty when the team at *Airliner World* find themselves at an airport. Our location at the time and distance from the airport tends to influence our method of transportation to it – do we use the train, the metro system, a bus, taxi, short or long-stay car park, cadge a lift or walk? Over time we've done the lot!

Of all the various ways of getting there, one thing that really seems to irk a lot of people these days is the drop-off charge. Some refer to it as the drop-off tax, it being like death and potholes… rather hard to avoid.

The point of the drop-off charge is to 'encourage' the general public to use public transport, which in a perfect world we probably all would. But the practicalities of life often prevent it, or make it unfeasibly difficult to achieve without some strategic forward thinking and faith in good fortune that the public transport system will operate in the way it was designed…

My local airport – Gatwick – is about 25 miles away and to use public transport to get there is more like an episode of *Race Across the World*. It's a 1.9-mile schlep to the station, which means I need to leave home bang on 5am to make the first train of the day at 5.42am – and after one change that gets to Gatwick at 7.04am if the network is running to time. For any flight leaving before 8am this strategy doesn't work, unless I make the journey the night before and stay in a hotel – I'm getting poorer with each strike of the keyboard! On Saturdays, the first train is at 6.44am and on Sundays it's 9.45am. Not good. The problem is reversed at the other end of the day, racing to board the last train for home before it leaves passengers stranded.

And as for the bus… that's 2hrs 40mins with four changes – frustrated emoji. The drop-off charge at £7, plus some petrol money for a willing friend is cheap and efficient by comparison.

Around the UK charges vary from £5-£7 at most airports, with Birmingham

being a beacon of freedom, albeit with a 500m walk. The intention is admirable, but the practicalities will only ever work for those close to a reliable, open most hours, public transport network. The airports say these charges can be avoided by using the free drop-off option most of them provide, usually located some distance from the terminal, followed by a bus ride, but this is just another logistical hurdle to factor into the journey. They also say the charges help fund infrastructure and public transport improvements. The problem is two-fold, a public transport system that only really works for a percentage of airport users, and a charge for others that's tricky to avoid.

And where the public transport system is far-reaching and operating most hours, the poor punter can be hit with premium pricing. Recently, I was invited to attend an event at Heathrow and merrily toddled off to the railway station at early o'clock as dawn broke. Once in central London, at Farringdon station I changed to the Elizabeth Line, grabbed a seat and began to relax for what was scheduled to be a 35-minute journey. A couple of stops later I looked up at the map and saw to my horror that I didn't

have the correct ticket for the spur line to Heathrow. I jumped off at Paddington, took a District Line to Earl's Court and then the clickety-clack of the Piccadilly Line, totalling a further 55 minutes and scraping in with barely a minute to spare. Of course, new infrastructure has to be paid for, but premium pricing forces some to seek alternatives, either by design or, in my case, by accident, when surely the point is to showcase its brilliance and effectiveness and move people efficiently. A few days earlier, I had been at Madrid/Barajas Terminal 4, where the metro ticket from arrivals to the city centre cost €7.50, and the taxi returning me to departures dropped me off with no drop-off charge. A breath of fresh Spanish air.

So what is the alternative? There's not much point increasing fees for airlines and airport concessions as they will likely be passed on to passengers. Airport car park prices can vary between reasonable and eye-watering, while eVTOL will operate for a minority not the majority. Cycling – not so easy with 23kg of hold luggage. Walking – same problem and slower still. It seems we're stuck in a holding pattern for the time being at least. I'll get my coat, but please let us know your thoughts…

It seems we're stuck in a holding pattern for the time being at least